SAVING FACE

The Art and History of the Goalie Mask

For my brother Mike, who brought me to hockey games back when masks had eyeholes... and for Jason and Sam, the next generation of Hynes hockey fanatics.

– J.H.

To the man who bought me my first fiberglass kit and lent me his tools to make my first mask, and who instilled in me a sense of passion for the game of hockey and for the written word—my father, Laurence Smith, who passed away during the writing of this book.

– G.S.

JIM HYNES AND GARY SMITH

SAVING FACE

The Art and History of the Goalie Mask

Foreword by Hockey Hall of Fame
Goaltender **GERRY CHEEVERS**

John Wiley & Sons Canada, Ltd.

Library and Archives Canada Cataloguing in Publication Data

Hynes, Jim

Saving face : the art and history of the goalie mask / Jim Hynes, Gary Smith.

Includes index.

ISBN 978-0-470-15558-5

1. Hockey masks. 2. Hockey masks—History. I. Smith, Gary, 1962–
III. Title.

GV848.78.M37 2008   796.962028'4   C2008-902116-9

Production Credits

Concept and Design: Griffintown Media (Jim McRae, President; Annic Lavertu, Vice-President)

Cover and interior text design: Philippe Arnoldi, Art Director; Judy Coffin, Designer

Printer: Quebecor–Taunton

John Wiley & Sons Canada, Ltd.
6045 Freemont Blvd.
Mississauga, Ontario
L5R 4J3

Printed in the United States

1 2 3 4 5 QW 12 11 10 09 08

Contents

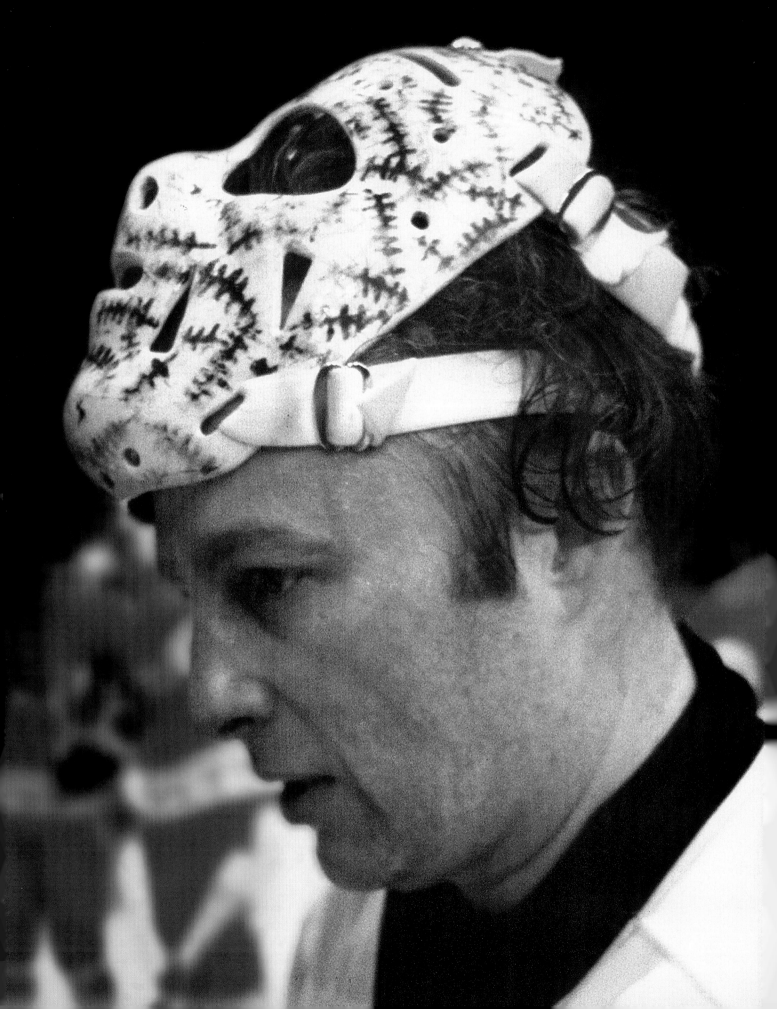

Foreword

HOW I SAVED MY OWN FACE

If you believe the people who care about these things, it seems that I am regarded as some sort of goalie mask pioneer. Well, that may be true, but I certainly didn't set out to be. In fact, I avoided wearing a mask as long as I could.

In a way, I guess I do qualify as some sort of authority on masks, because I played with one—and without one—in the NHL. My first two NHL games were with the Toronto Maple Leafs. The first was against the Chicago Blackhawks and Bobby Hull, who had the hardest shot in hockey at that time. And there was little ol' me, 21 years old and no mask. We won somehow and I played again the next night in Detroit. I'll never forget it: Gordie Howe came down the wing and wristed what I figured was a routine shot. Well, that routine shot knocked the stick out of my hand.

Even though it took me a few years and a few near misses to go out and get one, I finally realized that if I wanted to play in the NHL I would need to wear a mask. My first mask was made by Lefty Wilson, the trainer for the Detroit Red Wings. I didn't like it much—it moved around like crazy.

About a year later, a guy named Ernie Higgins came around the Bruins' dressing room. He had figured out a way of anchoring a mask to your chin so it wouldn't move. His mask was better than any other I had tried, but it still made it hard to see pucks at your feet. So even though it drove old Ernie crazy, I cut the mask's eyeholes even bigger. I ended up wearing an Ernie Higgins mask for the rest of my career.

I guess what I am really famous for are the stitch marks I used to put on my mask every time I got a puck in the face. Without those, my old Ernie Higgins mask wouldn't be on the cover of this book. It started as a bit of a joke, and you can read all about it on the pages inside, but I guess that was the start of mask art. And that is something else you can read all about in this story about the art and history of the goalie mask.

I hope you enjoy it.

GERRY CHEEVERS

May 2008, Boston, Massachusetts

Introduction

MASK APPEAL

Throughout history, humans have worn masks of all types and for different reasons. Cultures in just about every part of the world have used masks in rituals, ceremonies and celebrations. There were masks for war, masks for the hunt, masks to ward off evil spirits or to call upon friendly ones. There were even masks for entertainment, like those worn by ancient Greek and Japanese theater actors.

In some cases, masks are considered important works of art. In fact, one of the world's oldest masks, the 5,500-year-old Lady of Warka, is known as the Sumerian Mona Lisa. A 20-centimeter-high marble sculpture of a woman's head, the priceless work is one of the first sculpted depictions of the human face.

To a large degree, though, masks have served needs more utilitarian than artistic over the centuries, whether providing disguise or for administering torture (iron masks). Some, purposely hideous, were intended to gain advantage by frightening the wearer's enemies.

Although separated by millennia, it's not difficult to see the form of a goalie's mask in this mesolithic mask, c. 7,000 B.C.

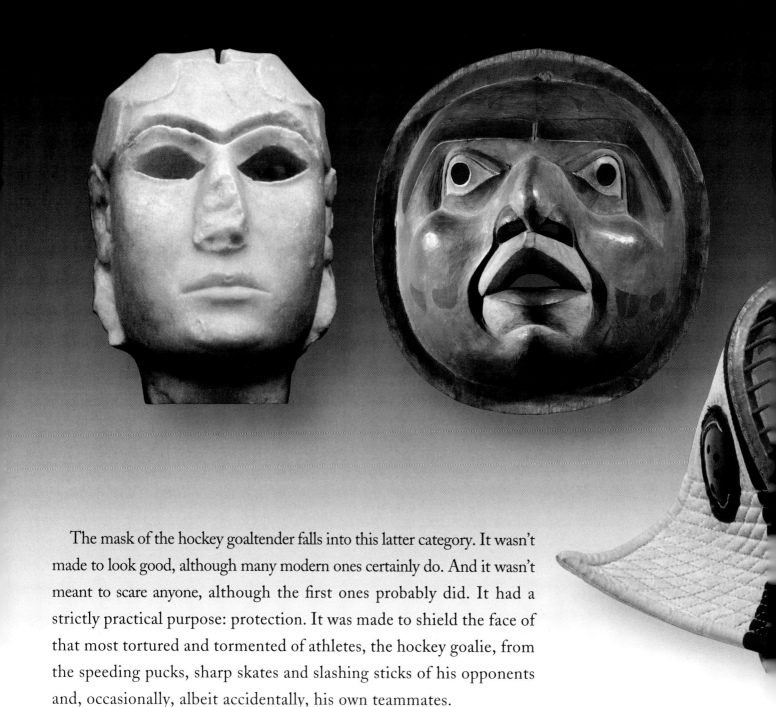

The mask of the hockey goaltender falls into this latter category. It wasn't made to look good, although many modern ones certainly do. And it wasn't meant to scare anyone, although the first ones probably did. It had a strictly practical purpose: protection. It was made to shield the face of that most tortured and tormented of athletes, the hockey goalie, from the speeding pucks, sharp skates and slashing sticks of his opponents and, occasionally, albeit accidentally, his own teammates.

GAME FACE

Unintentionally, the first goalie masks, as rudimentary in form and construction as they were, have become as compelling as the famous masks of art and war that preceded them... to hockey fans anyway.

As mask design and, indeed, art, advanced over the years, the goalie mask would begin to take on a mystique of its own, often transcending

Mask design has spanned ages and cultures, including the 5,500-year-old Lady of Warka mask and a West Coast native mask (above, left). Masks are most commonly used for protection, including the Japanese kendo mask, the Greek soldier's mask and the goalie mask (above, right), from the collection of New York's Museum of Modern Art.

the sport for which it was created. A plain white one made by American Ernest C. Higgins, better known as Ernie Higgins, can be found at New York's Museum of Modern Art. Canadian mask maker Greg Harrison's work was featured in a 1981 Kleinburg Museum exhibition, called Soultenders and Goaltenders, which presented goalie masks alongside West Coast native masks.

Still, it is the hockey fan who is most enamored of the goalie mask, both for the role it has played in the history of the game and for the story of its development—one of the most intriguing in all of hockey lore. The goalie mask has become not just another piece of protection, but the most recognizable and personalized piece of equipment in all of sport.

Until now, however, even though hundreds of hockey books have been written—a good number of them about goalies—no book has been dedicated to the goalie's other face—his saving face. Here is the story of the goalie mask.

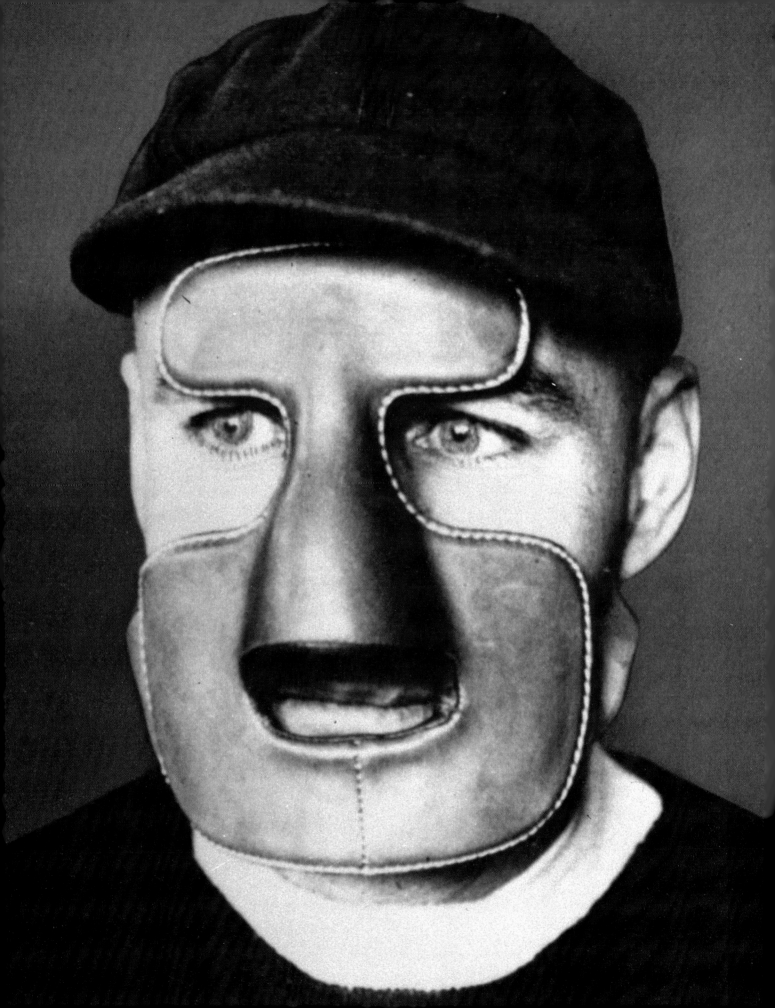

Chapter One

THE INNOVATORS

Nicknamed "Praying Benny" for his habit of dropping to the ice to make a save, goalie Clint Benedict wore this crude leather and wire mask in a 1930 NHL game after a Howie Morenz shot broke his nose and cheekbone earlier that season.

The slapshot and curved sticks were still decades away, but by 1930 injuries to goaltenders were nevertheless a growing concern... to goaltenders, if to no one else. Clint Benedict, an eventual Hall of Fame goalie and four-time Stanley Cup champion, had only himself to blame for this. The strapping, wily veteran had earned the nickname "Praying Bennie" in the early years of the 20th century by spending much of the game on his knees to stop pucks from getting past him, even though it was illegal in the NHL at that time for goalies to drop to the ice to make a save. Benedict would simply argue that he had fallen by accident, and he would usually avoid the two-minute penalty the infraction carried. Finally, in 1918, NHL president Frank Calder, driven to distraction at seeing his referees unable to distinguish between a real or fake Benedict tumble, eliminated the rule prohibiting goalies from dropping to the ice. Netminders were now free to spend as much time as they wanted lying down on the job, closer to the ever-present dangers lurking there.

Between the time of its tentative first steps in the late 19th century and the birth of the National Hockey League in 1917, the game of hockey changed significantly. Equipment improved, players grew more skilled, and rules were changed to make the game faster and more dynamic. Positions, and the way they were played, changed too. Defensemen, for example, never strayed from their end of the rink during hockey's formative years. Meanwhile, the position of rover (a free-roaming skill player) was eliminated altogether by the early 1920s.

Goaltenders were not immune to change. Some goalies liked to wander more than others, skating out of their crease to clear away pucks. But for the most part, goalies stayed put in front of their net. One thing is for sure though: even after equipment developments such as protective leg

The earliest hockey games featured netless goals and maskless tenders who played mainly upright between two pegs.

pads and catching gloves were added around the turn of the 20th century, goalies played the game standing up. In many leagues, the rules of the game actually prohibited them from dropping to the ice.

In those days, the puck rarely left the ice. Players' sticks were heavy and rigid, with thick, straight blades. Lifting the puck was uncommon, not an important part of the game—and difficult to achieve intentionally, too. For the most part, shots on goal were whipped along the ice, so there was no need for the goaltender to use anything but the blade of his stick to block a shot on goal. Yes, goalies were smart but also practical fellows back in the early days of hockey. They didn't drop down because they really didn't need to. And, after all, why should they go low and put themselves in the line of fire?

Since goalies' faces were not often in harm's way, there was no need to protect them. Or so logic dictated. Then along came Clint Benedict to change all that.

PRAYING BENNY

A professional since joining the Ottawa Senators in 1912, Clint Benedict had already earned the nicknames "Praying Benny" and "Tumbling Clint" by the time the NHL was formed. By then, hockey had emerged as a way of making money, although not a particularly honorable one in the eyes of many. The new National Hockey League was full of promise for aspiring professionals. But with only four teams actually playing games in the inaugural 1917–18 season (one of whom, the Montreal Wanderers, played in just six games before a devastating fire at their home rink caused them to drop out), there were actually less than a handful of goaltending jobs to go around. There was no such thing as a backup goaltender back then.

Competition for goaltending jobs was fierce. So if risks needed to be taken to secure one of them, then Clint Benedict was ready to take them, diving and sprawling along the ice to make saves. The practice of dropping down was permitted in other pro leagues, but not in the NHL. Trouble was, the two-minute penalty for hitting the ice to make a save was based on intent, and by 1918 Clint Benedict had perfected the "accidental fall."

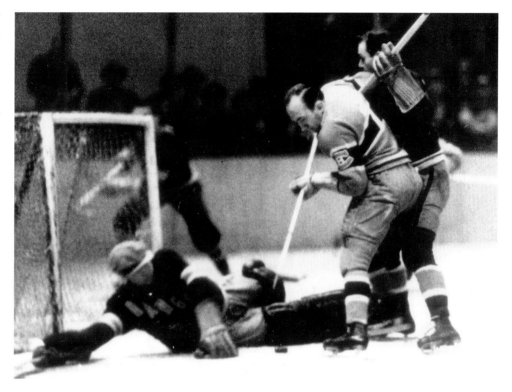

Montreal Canadiens legend Howie Morenz scored 40 goals in the 1929–30 season. He also injured Maroons goalie Clint Benedict twice that year with shots to the face and neck.

"What you had to be was sneaky," Benedict told an interviewer just months before his death in 1976. "You'd make a move, fake losing your balance or footing, and put the officials on the spot—did I fall down, or did I intentionally go down?"

NHL referees couldn't tell the difference, but some hockey purists could, and derided the practice. On January 9, 1918, unable to stomach the blatant rule infringement any longer, NHL president Frank Calder simply dropped the rule itself.

"In the future they can fall on their knees or stand on their heads if they think they can stop the puck better in that way than by standing on their feet," Calder told newspaper reporters. (This is perhaps the origin of the expression "stood on his head," now commonly used to describe an outstanding goaltending performance.)

Clint Benedict's perfecting of the "accidental fall" led to a 1918 rule change which finally allowed goaltenders to drop to the ice to make a save.

Now operating within the rules, Benedict began to perfect his technique. He finished last in goals against average (GAA) with a 5.12 mark in 1917–18, but was the leading NHL goalie in both GAA and shutouts for the next five seasons, topping the likes of Montreal Canadiens great Georges Vézina along the way. In 1923–24, he finished second, posting a 1.99 GAA to Vézina's 1.97. During those years, Benedict helped his Senators claim three Stanley Cup titles. He then moved to the Montreal Maroons in 1924–25, and delivered a Stanley Cup to his new team the following season.

Dropping down to make a save served Benedict well, but it also led to injuries for him and those who followed him down to the ice surface. To beat the prone goalie, players were resorting more and more to—borrowing a phrase from pond hockey—"lifters." And this meant more pucks to the face of the still maskless marvels of the net.

THE FIRST MASK

Midway through the 1929–30 season, Benedict took a hard shot to the head while diving to make a save against Boston's Dit Clapper. A few days later, on January 7, 1930, he was struck in the face by a screened blast from Canadiens superstar Howie Morenz. Knocked unconscious by the shot, Benedict awoke in hospital, his nose badly broken and cheekbone shattered.

Benedict was out of the Maroons line-up for the next six weeks. When he finally returned to action for a February 22 game against the New York Americans at Madison Square Garden, he was wearing a strange-looking mask to protect his still-healing face. An article in the February 23, 1930 edition of the *New York Times* noted: "Benedict, the Maroons goalie, played his first game since his injuries over a month ago, wearing a huge mask to protect his injured nose."

The first mask worn in an NHL game bore no resemblance to those that followed some 30 years later. Manufactured by a Boston sporting

The origin of the mask Clint Benedict wore in 1930 NHL action is unknown. Some say it was a football face guard, others say it was a boxer's sparring mask.

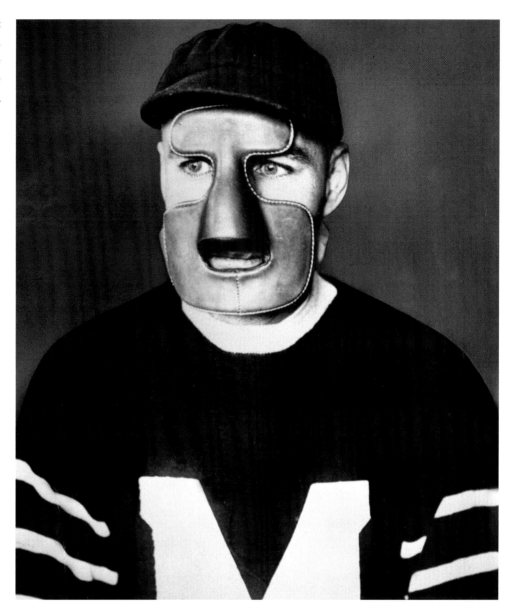

goods company, it has been described as both a football face guard and a boxer's sparring mask. Made of leather and supported by wire, it protected the forehead, mouth and especially the nose, but not the eyes. The large nosepiece obscured Benedict's vision, causing him to discard the mask soon after that first game, which ended in a 3–3 tie. It is unclear exactly how many times Benedict wore the mask. Different sources give different answers, varying from one to five games. Some say Benedict shelved it permanently after a 2–1 loss to the Chicago Blackhawks, a loss he blamed directly on the mask. Benedict's season ended for good a few weeks later after another Morenz shot hit him in the throat during a

Maroons-Canadiens contest on March 4. He had played only 14 games in that, his final NHL season.

Clint Benedict may have been the first NHLer to wear a mask in a game, but a number of amateur hockey goalies had donned face masks several years before him. There is evidence to show that the practice of wearing masks was fairly common the further you got from the high-stakes, macho world of pro hockey, where coaches would argue that wearing a mask would impede vision, or worse, indicate that the goalie wearing it lacked one of the key elements required to play the position: courage.

The baseball catcher's mask (see *Tool of Ingenuity: The Thayer Mask*, page 22) was invented by Harvard man Fred Thayer in 1877, and it is more than plausible that hockey goalies would have worn one soon after it became widely available in sporting goods stores. In fact, we know that goaltenders did just that a few decades later. The Hockey Hall of Fame in Toronto has photographs of an anonymous North American goaltender in Switzerland wearing a catcher's-type mask sometime in the late 1920s, while another photograph shows Japan's goalie, Teiji Honma, wearing a more modern catcher's mask at the 1936 Winter Olympics at Garmisch-Partenkirchen, Germany.

Japanese goalie Teiji Honma wore a cage-type mask at the 1936 Olympics, while Roy Musgrove wore a half cage playing in England.

A mask similar to the one worn by Roy Musgrove while playing in the British National Hockey League.

LADIES FIRST?

There is also evidence that the first ever mask-wearing goaltender may have been a woman. In 1927, Elizabeth Graham, the principal puck-stopper on the Queen's University women's hockey team, "gave the fans a surprise when she stepped into the nets and then donned a fencing mask," according to a report in the *Montreal Daily Star*. One story has it that Graham's father made her wear the mask after she had sustained serious damage to her teeth while playing goal.

Despite Elizabeth Graham's choice of protection, the metal bars of the catcher's mask were soon favored over the fine mesh of the fencing mask. Indeed, the catcher's mask was often worn by goaltenders who needed to wear eyeglasses. As twisted as it may seem today, the logic of the time seemed to be that it was perfectly reasonable to play goalie

The Thayer Mask

For years, the baseball catcher's equipment was collectively referred to as "the tools of ignorance," presumably because nobody of sound mind would crouch behind home plate, trying to catch a hard, speeding ball while someone standing in front of him tried to hit it with a piece of lumber. Foul tips are as old as the game itself. So, before the invention of the catcher's mask, you had to be about as crazy as a hockey goalie to play catcher in a baseball game.

Fred Thayer, the player-manager of the Harvard Baseball Club in the 1870s, was having a hard time finding anyone brave and/or crazy enough to play catcher on his team. His best prospect for the position, future major leaguer James Tyng, had caught a few games, but had become "gun shy" after getting hit with a few foul tips. Thayer, who had seen an opposing catcher wearing a fencing mask with eye holes cut in it the previous year, set to work developing a mask for catchers. He designed a mask with sturdier metal bars and wider spaces for better vision and commissioned a Cambridge, Massachusetts, tinsmith to make it. The finished product came complete with padded chin and forehead rests to cushion the blows from baseballs. James Tyng debuted the mask in the spring of 1877. *The Harvard Crimson* newspaper called it "a complete success," which "adds greatly to the confidence of the catcher, who need not feel that he is every moment in danger of a life-long injury. To the ingenious inventor of this mask we are largely indebted for the excellent playing of our new catcher, who promises to excel the fine playing of those who have previously held this position."

Others mocked the new piece of equipment and questioned the courage of the man who wore it, but the mask quickly caught on. Thayer patented his invention in 1878. Later that year, the A.G. Spalding and Brothers sporting goods company began selling both Thayer's Patent Harvard Baseball Mask, as well as a similar version of their own design, for $3.

without a mask and risk losing your eye, but that breaking your glasses was to be avoided at all costs. The bespectacled Roy Musgrove wore what has been described as a field lacrosse mask while playing in the British National Hockey League from 1936 to 1939 for the Wembley Lions—a team coached by none other than Clint Benedict. Similar to a cage, it was actually a half-mask that protected only the eyes. Years later, future Hockey Hall of Famer Tony Esposito would wear a catcher's mask while tending the nets on rinks near his home in Sault Ste. Marie, Ontario, to protect his face… and his glasses.

TORTURED HEROES

While amateur goalies were starting to protect their faces, professional netminders continued to tempt fate by going maskless. And many paid a steep price for it, suffering both physically and mentally. While their opponents' increasingly hard shots were shattering facial bones, it was the fear of injury and the pressure to succeed that shattered goalies' nerves. The title of a 1967 book by Toronto sportswriter Jim Hunt says it all: *The Men in the Nets: Hockey's Tortured Heroes.*

Goaltending legend Glenn Hall would become physically ill, vomiting before every game, sometimes between periods, and after the game was over, too. Hall, whose nerves and disposition got worse with each passing season, came to hate his job, and threatened to quit many times over the course of his long career. "I sometimes ask myself 'what the hell I am doing out here,'" he said in 1967. "But it's the only way I can support my family. If I could do it some other way I wouldn't be playing goal."

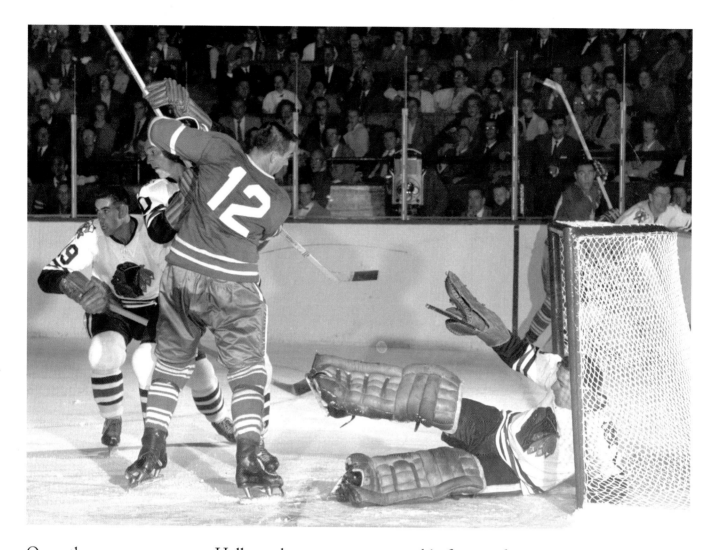

Once the season was over, Hall was known to retreat to his farm and scream in an empty field until he felt better. During his days with the St. Louis Blues, Hall would leave the team hanging until just before training camp before committing to another season. Hall also famously used the excuse of having to paint his barn to explain his late arrival in St. Louis one year. When Blues coach Scotty Bowman surprised Hall by dropping in at the farm, he found his goalie drinking a bottle of beer on his front porch... but no barn in sight.

Hall was not alone in letting the job make him physically ill. Jacques Plante was also frequently sick to his stomach, and also suffered from asthma—although his detractors, which included his own coaches, would dismiss his ills as hypochondria. Others, such as Toronto Maple Leafs keeper Frank "Ulcers" McCool, developed stomach problems.

The great Glenn Hall would sometimes question the logic of playing the rough-and-tumble position of goaltender.

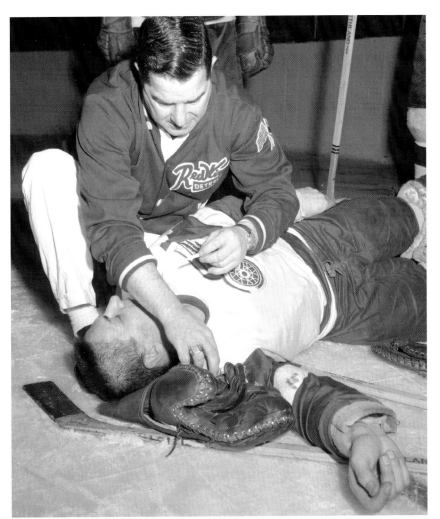

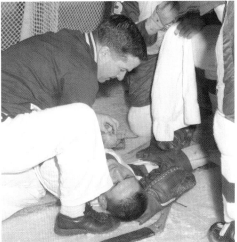

Terry Sawchuk was often caught in the dangerous mix of skates, sticks and pucks. Famed trainer Lefty Wilson is shown giving emergency care.

Many goalies before and after him could have shared his unfortunate nickname. Roger Crozier, the Detroit Red Wings goalie through much of the 1960s, was said to have ulcers when he was 17, even before he played in the NHL.

Many goalies, such as Terry Sawchuk, turned to alcohol to steady themselves. Others, such as McCool, Montreal's Wilf Cude, Bill Durnan and Gerry McNeil (Jacques Plante's predecessor in the Canadiens goal), burned out before their time, unable to withstand the stress any longer. Terry Sawchuk walked out on the Boston Bruins midway through the 1956–57 season, only to return the following year for Detroit. A few goalies, such as the seemingly doomed Sawchuk and Chicago Blackhawks star Charlie Gardiner, died shockingly young. Most, however, played on through the fear and the pain, since

there were only six decent goaltending jobs in the world at that time and, despite the dangers, plenty of competition for the spots.

Gerry McNeil preceded Jacques Plante in goal for the Canadiens in a career derailed by the stresses of the position.

STICKS AND PUCKS MAY BREAK MY BONES

Many pre-mask goaltenders used dark humor to cope with the very real prospect of getting gravely injured. Most told stories about losing their "chiclets" (teeth) or the number of stitches (which they glibly called "zippers") they'd received in their face. Scars and broken facial bones were worn like a grim badge of honor by the members of the goaltending brotherhood. Asked why he always shaved the day of a

Frank "Ulcers" McCool carried a nickname that belied his surname.

game, Toronto Maple Leafs great Lorne Chabot replied, "Because I stitch better when my skin is smooth."

Most people today would find nothing remotely funny about the injuries these goalies suffered and the pain they suffered through. Most pre-mask goalies received hundreds of stitches in their face and head. Broken jaws and cheekbones were common, too. Johnny Bower claims to have received more than 200 stitches, the same number as Jacques Plante, who also had his nose broken four times, his jaw broken once and both cheekbones fractured in the 10 or so years he played without a mask. Plante also suffered a hairline fracture of his skull.

Not only did maskless goalies suffer horrific injuries, they actually continued to play with their injuries. With no backup goalies waiting on the end of the bench to fill in, injured goalies were hauled into dressing rooms or crude arena infirmaries to undergo emergency repairs, usually without anesthetic.

During the 1960–61 season, Lorne "Gump" Worsley of the New York Rangers was knocked unconscious after getting hit in the left eye with a hard shot, and only came to while he was being stitched up in the Rangers' dressing room. When Rangers coach Alfie Pike asked if he could continue, the still woozy Worsley replied "sure" and headed back out onto the ice, despite the fact that he could only see out of his right eye.

A few years later, Boston Bruins goalie Eddie Johnston had his nose broken three times in one week. The first time, a doctor in New York's Madison Square Garden stuck his fingers up Johnston's nose and tweaked it back into place so that it would not impede his vision. The next night he was struck again, and needed 12 stitches to close a gash. Two days later, he broke his nose again in Montreal. The pain was excruciating, but each time he headed back out onto the ice. Johnston dared not take a night off, because he knew, as every NHL goalie at the time did, that the minor leagues were full of young goalies waiting for their chance to play in the NHL... and take his job in the process. Johnston ended up breaking his nose seven times during his 17-year NHL career, much of which he played with a mask.

The Leafs' Lorne Chabot liked to be clean-shaven so he could stitch better.

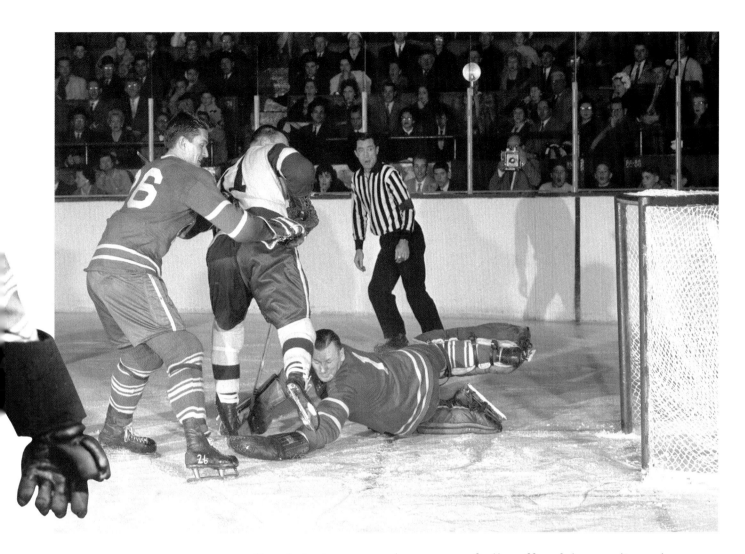

Hall of Famer Johnny Bower wasn't shy to put his nose in the action.

Eye injuries were the worst of all suffered by goalies, the most serious of them ending careers on the spot, not to mention causing permanent loss of sight. One of the most infamous eye injuries was suffered by Terry Sawchuk in 1947, his rookie season in pro hockey. While Sawchuk was playing with Omaha of the United States Hockey League, his great career was almost over before it began when a stick sliced through his right eyeball during a goalmouth scramble. The first prognosis was permanent, irreparable damage, and plans were made to remove the eye the following day. But as luck would have it, a surgeon passing through town asked to have another look. Legend, and Sawchuk's autobiography, says that the young goaltender's eyeball was removed, repaired with three stitches, and then returned to his eye socket. It was his 18th birthday.

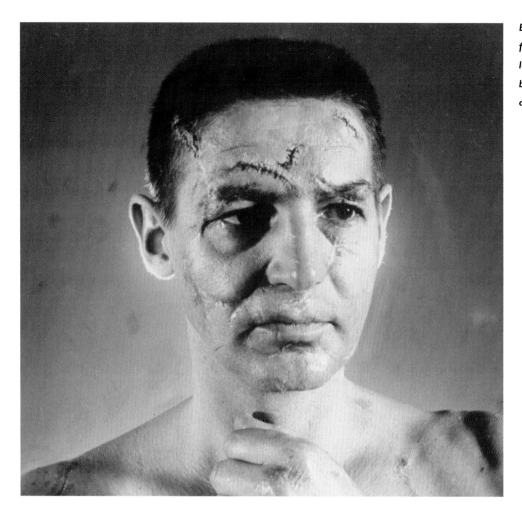

The eye injury was but the first in a long line of serious injuries for Sawchuk, who, according to some sources, received as many as 600 stitches in his face as well as two broken noses, punctured lungs, a broken instep and ruptured discs in his back as a result of playing goal. In 1966, a prominent magazine featured a photo of Sawchuk, with the stitches on his face enhanced to be more prominent. The result looked something like an early sci-fi villain: half-human, half-alien and brutally unhappy. Often called the greatest goaltender of all time, Sawchuk died in 1970 at the age of 40, a physical and mental wreck.

THE LOUCH MASK

NHL goalies first started experimenting with goalie masks in the mid-1950s, albeit only during practices. That Montreal's Jacques Plante was one of the first to don a mask was no surprise to hockey

Hockey legend and mask pioneer Jacques Plante was no stranger to the trainer's table.

followers. Plante, a pioneer in terms of goaltending technique, was also known for having a mind of his own, a trait that often saw him at odds with those who coached him.

Plante debuted with Montreal in 1952–53, playing in three games, then played 17 more in 1953–54 in relief of the increasingly fragile Gerry McNeil. By 1954–55, he was Montreal's full-time goalie, and almost immediately began toying with the idea of wearing a face mask. He may have tried a plastic one sent to him by a Granby, Quebec, man as early as 1954, and old photos show him with a variety of other kinds of masks, including a catcher's-type cage and a lacrosse-type half mask.

That same year, a St. Marys, Ontario, inventor named Delbert Louch created the precursor to today's visor, a clear plastic, full-face shield he marketed as the "shatterproof face protector for all sports."

Jacques Plante modified his
Delbert Louch shield for better
vision, comfort and protection.

Louch sent one of his masks to each of the NHL's six starting goaltenders. Gump Worsley of the New York Rangers, who history has shown never met a mask he didn't hate, complained that the new shield was too warm, and that the glare it reflected from the arena lights, combined with its tendency to fog up, obscured his vision. Terry Sawchuk and Detroit Red Wings general manager Jack Adams at first endorsed the Louch mask, which was soon adopted by youth hockey associations across Canada and the United States. Photos exist of Sawchuk wearing one in a Red Wings practice, but it appears that he soon set it aside. Toronto goalie Johnny Bower did the same, but not before posing for a photograph with it on.

Toronto's Johnny Bower sported a clear plastic Louch mask for this photo, but never for a game.

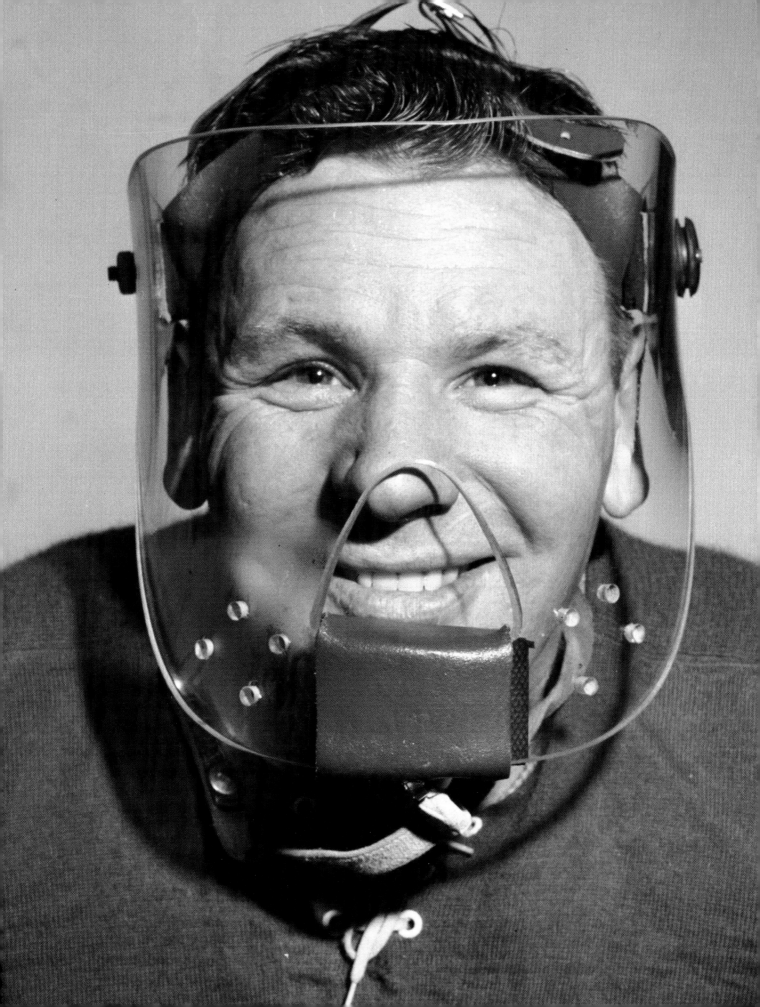

Jacques Plante had the same complaints about the Louch mask that Worsley and the others had. But instead of giving up on it, Plante modified the mask, cutting a large eye opening and contouring its sides to improve visibility. Even though Plante used the mask in practice for several years, Delbert Louch's shield never made it into an NHL game.

RESISTANCE

The Louch mask was far from perfect. But Plante and others may have used it in games anyway—had certain attitudes of the day not prevented them from doing so. Even by the late 1950s, a netminder wanting to wear a mask would have had to fight his way through a minefield of resistance. The attitudes of their coaches, teammates and fans now seem archaic, but they were a matter of fact for professional goalies in the 1930s, '40s and '50s.

The last people who wanted to see masked goaltenders in pro hockey games were coaches and general managers, who, at that time, were also responsible for ticket sales. Backed by a litany of excuses and arguments, most of which ring hollow today, they refused to let their goaltenders wear masks in games. Their attacks ranged from criticisms of the mask designs ("You can't see a puck at your feet"; "They're too heavy"; "They're too hot") to amateur psychology ("Goalies need fear to be on edge, it keeps them alert"; "Without a mask, a goalie will be too complacent") to attacks on pride and manhood ("A real man wouldn't hide his face from his opponents"). And then there was the financial argument: "The goaltenders in our organization will never wear a mask," said New York Rangers general manager Muzz Patrick. Why? "Because women who like hockey want to see the players' faces."

THE FIBERGLASS REVOLUTION

In 1958, Montrealer Bill Burchmore was 35 years old and the sales manager for a company called Fibreglass Canada Ltd. The long-time youth hockey coach and Montreal Canadiens fan was in the stands at the Montreal Forum when Jacques Plante was struck in the forehead during a playoff game against the Boston Bruins. The game was delayed for 45 minutes while doctors stitched up the gash in Plante's head. At work the next day, Burchmore found himself staring at a mannequin's head, recalling the events of the previous evening. The mannequin was made of fiberglass.

Fiberglass, which is essentially glass-reinforced plastic, was invented during the Second World War. It was first used widely in boat building in the 1950s. Easily molded, and very hard after setting, it soon had numerous commercial uses. Burchmore was convinced that he could design a fiberglass mask, molded to fit the contours of a goaltender's face like a second skin. The mask would be light but strong, and molding it to fit the face would help ensure it didn't hinder the goalie's vision.

For more than a year, Burchmore experimented, eventually coming up with the process to make such a mask. Finally, shortly after the Canadiens won their fourth consecutive Stanley Cup in the spring of 1959, he wrote Jacques Plante a letter explaining his idea for a mask.

BILL BURCHMORE: Mr. Fiberglass

If a single individual can be credited with having invented the goalie mask, then that person would be Montrealer Bill Burchmore. Others before him made protective face masks for goalies. But those masks all had flaws that stopped NHL goalies from using them outside of practices. It is the fiberglass mask, and Burchmore's way of manufacturing it, that finally broke through and began to be used in NHL games. It remained the mask of choice for most goaltenders for a quarter century.

Having witnessed Montreal Canadiens goaltender Jacques Plante crumple to the ice after taking a puck to the face in a 1958 playoff game, and inspired by a fiberglass mannequin at his place of work, Fibreglass Canada Ltd., Burchmore, a 35-year-old sales manager, was convinced that fiberglass was the right material for the task at hand. Easily molded when soft, it became extremely hard when it dried.

Burchmore started experimenting with various mask-making methods, at one point practicing the art of face mold making on a young colleague named Al McKinney. Claustrophobic, McKinney nevertheless agreed to have his eyes covered, straws inserted in his nose, and plaster of Paris slathered over his face.

Burchmore soon perfected his method, which involved covering the face molds with layers of fiberglass sheets soaked in polyester resin, and letting them harden. The mask he made for Plante, the one the Canadiens goalie was wearing the night he made hockey history in 1959 (see page 38) weighed 14 ounces and was 3/16th of an inch thick.

Plante had been wearing Bill Burchmore's mask for only three months when Burchmore came up with another innovation. By January of 1960, he had designed a mask using fiberglass yarn instead of

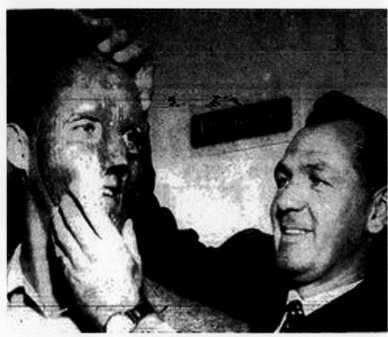

The right fit: Bill Burchmore's fiberglass mask was both welcomed and widely used by a generation of goalies.

sheets. And Plante was once again a willing "guinea pig" for the new design, called a "bar" or "pretzel" mask because it resembled a twisted pretzel. The new mask, which weighed only 10.3 ounces, was a dark caramel tone, the color of the polyester resin used. Some said it looked like giant worms crawling on Plante's face. However unsightly, the pretzel mask did allow for better ventilation, which at the time was the biggest complaint amongst the goaltenders who were experimenting with masks. Burchmore continued to make pretzel masks throughout the 1960s. His customers included NHL goalies like Cesare Maniago and Charlie Hodge, and countless junior, senior league and minor pro goalies. Burchmore made two pretzel masks for Plante. The legendary goaltender wore his second pretzel mask, which was somewhat larger than the first one, when he came out of retirement to join the St. Louis Blues in 1968.

Plante was reluctant at first. He knew what his coach, Hector "Toe" Blake, thought about masks and anyone who wanted to wear one. Perhaps the idea of having a plaster face mold made wasn't exactly appealing either. But sometime in the summer of 1959, Plante, accompanied by Canadiens team doctor Ian Milne and trainer Bill Head, made his way to the Montreal General Hospital to have a mold made. Plante had to wear a woman's nylon stocking over his head and cover his face with Vaseline. Straws were inserted in his nose to allow him to breathe while his face was slathered with plaster of Paris.

Plante's face mold was then sent to Burchmore, who quickly got to work layering sheets of fiberglass cloth saturated with polyester resin. The result was a 14-ounce, 1/8th-inch-thick mask able to withstand tremendous impact. For comfort and padding, Burchmore glued thin strips of rubber to the inside of the mask at the forehead, cheekbones and chin. Adjustable leather straps attached to the sides secured it to the head. In an attempt to disguise its presence, Burchmore painted the mask in a so-called flesh tone.

Plante tried the mask out in the training camp that soon followed and immediately fell in love with it for the protection it provided him. He swore that he could see perfectly well with it on. Toe Blake and others in the Canadiens front office were not so sure. Blake told Plante that he could wear the mask in practice but that doing so in a game would be a bad idea. He argued that if things went badly and Plante let in a few soft goals, people would blame the mask. Over the long run, Blake reasoned, wearing a mask could compromise Plante's chances of winning a record

NOVEMBER 1, 1959:
Enter the Mask

A Canadian Heritage Minute television spot was made to commemorate it, and a children's book in which it features prominently (*The Goalie Mask* by Mike Leonetti) has become a bestseller. And in 2007, 48 years after it happened, *The Hockey News* magazine ranked Jacques Plante's debut of the molded fiberglass goalie mask at Madison Square Garden on November 1, 1959, fourth in a special edition chronicling "Sixty Moments That Changed The Game."

The story has been told and re-told countless times. And, like any good legend, it has grown to mythical proportions over the years. Early in the first period of a game between the New York Rangers and the defending Stanley Cup Champion Montreal Canadiens, a backhand shot delivered by Rangers star Andy Bathgate caught Montreal goalie Jacques Plante in the face, opening a savage cut along his nose. It has always been accepted that Bathgate hit Plante by accident. However, many years later, Andy Bathgate himself told Hockey Hall of Fame broadcaster Dick Irvin Jr. that he actually hit Plante on purpose, flicking the puck high, without too much on it, because he was angry with Plante over a previous altercation they'd had.

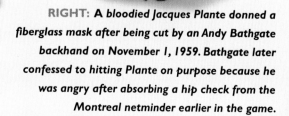

RIGHT: A bloodied Jacques Plante donned a fiberglass mask after being cut by an Andy Bathgate backhand on November 1, 1959. Bathgate later confessed to hitting Plante on purpose because he was angry after absorbing a hip check from the Montreal netminder earlier in the game.

Nevertheless, we know that Plante fell to the ice and was guided toward the Garden clinic, where Rangers team doctor Kazuo Yanagisawa ("Dr. Kamikaze" to the many players he stitched up) closed the ugly gash with seven stitches. Almost as ugly was the exchange between Plante and Canadiens coach Toe Blake after the Montreal goalie insisted that he would only return to action if he could wear the fiberglass mask he'd been wearing in practices. Blake finally relented, and Plante made his way to the Canadiens dressing room to fetch the mask.

When he skated back onto the ice at the start of play some 45 minutes after being hit, a hush fell over the Garden faithful as they witnessed what appeared to be Plante's exposed skull. To sportswriters of little imagination, Plante "looked like something right out of a Hollywood horror show." And to at least one critic, more cultured than the rest, he "looked like a character in a Japanese Noh play." "Plante looks like a man who has died from the neck up," wrote one wag. "Does Plante realize that he startles elderly ladies and frightens children?" questioned another.

By the time the final buzzer sounded on this historic night, the Rangers had put only one puck behind hockey's newly masked marvel. The Canadiens, meanwhile, deposited three behind one of the greatest mask resisters of them all, Rangers goalie Gump Worsley. Plante left the Garden that night with an understanding with Blake. He could continue to wear the mask until his injury healed. Later on they agreed that Plante could keep wearing the mask as long as the team was winning. And win they did.

For years, Plante's achievement was taken to be more important than Clint Benedict's brief experiment with a mask because it was said that he never again played without one. But that too is more fiction than fact. The truth is, Plante would indeed make one more maskless foray onto NHL ice.

ABOVE: *Jacques Plante used his original "flesh-colored" mask for less than half a season, switching to the lighter and cooler "pretzel" mask he designed with his mask-making collaborator Bill Burchmore in early 1960. He wore the mask until his first retirement in 1965, and again when he returned to the NHL in 1968.*

fifth-straight Vezina Trophy for being the NHL's top goaltender, not to mention the Canadiens' bid for a fifth-straight Stanley Cup. Plante reluctantly agreed to begin the 1959–60 season bare-faced once more.

ANOTHER BROADWAY DEBUT

The four-time defending Stanley Cup champion Canadiens got off to a fine start in the fall of 1959. The team was on an eight-game winning streak when it rolled into New York's Madison Square Garden on November 1 to take on the Rangers, who were led by star Andy Bathgate, the NHL's third-leading scorer the previous season. Three minutes into the game, posted about 10 feet from the Canadiens' net, Bathgate launched a backhand shot, the most difficult shot for goaltenders to anticipate. The rising shot struck Plante in the face, knocking him to the ice. Plante was cut, and Canadiens team trainers rushed him into the clinic in the Garden for repairs.

While a doctor was adding seven more stitches to Plante's already impressive facial collection, Montreal coach Toe Blake nervously paced the halls, even inquiring about the quality of the amateur backup goalies in the Garden crowd that night. Unimpressed, he called on Plante, who told him he would only return to the net if he could wear his mask. Plante was adamant, and Blake was in no position to argue with him. Forty-five minutes after getting hit, Plante skated back onto the Garden ice before a hushed crowd, wearing his ghostly-looking mask. Bathgate's backhander truly was a shot heard 'round the hockey world. Nobody knew it yet, but that shot, and the chain of events it set in motion, would change goaltending forever.

Jacques Plante's Bill Burchmore created mask is "The Mask" to many. It is arguably the single most important existing hockey artifact.

Chapter Two

THE GOLDEN AGE

The Andy Bathgate shot that sent Jacques Plante to the dressing room in search of his mask helped change the game of hockey forever. Following the lead of Montrealer Bill Burchmore, other would-be mask makers soon took to their workshops, working with plaster and fiberglass to try to build a better mask. After Plante's success with his mask, more and more goaltenders were willing to sit through a face mold-making session if the end result meant better protection.

The 1960s began with only two NHL goalies wearing masks, and many in the game, including some star goaltenders themselves, were critical of the mask. But by the end of the decade, bare-faced goalies would be in the minority. The greatest change of all was in the attitude of hockey's managers, who began to see the mask as protection for their investments rather than a coward's shield. Some NHL teams ordered all of the goalies in their system to start wearing masks. Improvements to mask making came with each passing year, and by the 1970s bigger, more protective masks were being made and even mass manufactured for goalies of all ages and levels. Things would eventually come full circle as Jacques Plante would once again play a critical role in the development of the goalie mask.

The first of the two "pretzel" masks Montrealer Bill Burchmore made for Canadiens goaltender Jacques Plante. Plante wore it for parts of two seasons in the early 1960s.

The day after debuting with it, Jacques Plante and his new mask were the talk of the hockey world. While reporters had tended to ignore Plante and other goalies' experiments with masks in practice, this new mask was big news. Bill Burchmore was big news, too. On December 12, 1959, he was the subject of a *Montreal Gazette* article by sportswriter Pat Curran under the headline "Mount Royal Inventor Comes to Goalies' Aid." In it, Burchmore proclaimed that Plante's mask would "eliminate 99 per cent of injuries," and also explained how Plante was confused about the kind of mask he was proposing.

"Jacques thought that I'd perfected the cage-type mask," Burchmore said. "He didn't understand plastics and thought I was crazy when I told him it would have to be molded if it was going to be any good. As a matter of fact, just about everyone thought I had rocks in my head."

Jacques Plante, Bill Burchmore and the mask they made famous were big news in 1959.

Boston Bruins goaltender Don Simmons was the second goalie in NHL history to wear a mask.

Burchmore brushed off the monster jokes and other criticisms of the mask's lack of aesthetic appeal, saying, "I designed the mask for protection, not for good looks. It has all of Jacques Plante's facial features. If it was made for Clark Gable, it would look like Clark Gable."

The article recounts how other goalies were ordering masks from Burchmore, which he said cost $300, and also offered the intriguing news that "Burchmore has also been contacted for details by the Russian Embassy" …whatever that meant.

Within weeks, other goalies were wearing masks in games. Gil Mayer of the American Hockey League's (AHL) Cleveland Barons later said that he received a mask from Jacques Plante himself after he broke his jaw in a game. Back in the NHL, Don Simmons of the Boston Bruins started wearing a fiberglass mask.

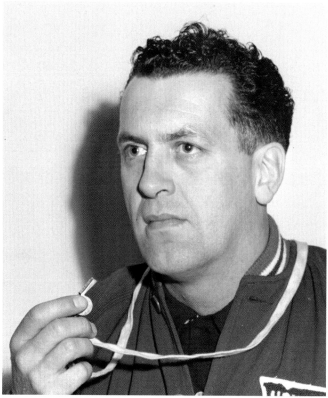

University of Alberta Golden Bears' netminder Gerry Schultz was one of the first goalies after Plante to don a mask. In 1960, a local newspaper dubbed him a "Poor Man's Plante." Schultz made the mask himself, using materials from the University's dental lab. He went on to become one of the most sought-after mask makers in Western Canada, especially by Junior A and Senior A goaltenders. One notable goalie who wore a couple of Schultz's creations in his first two seasons with the Edmonton Oilers was Grant Fuhr.

The mask had broken through, most critically, perhaps, with coaches, general managers and other officials. "We're anxious for goalies to wear anything that will cut down on injuries," said NHL President Clarence Campbell. Murray "Muzz" Patrick, the New York Rangers general manager who once swore that no goalie of his would wear a mask because female hockey fans wanted to see players' faces, soon changed his tune. He ordered all of the junior and juvenile goalies in the Rangers' system to start wearing masks, saying, "I'm convinced that the masks are here to stay. Our young players might as well get used to them."

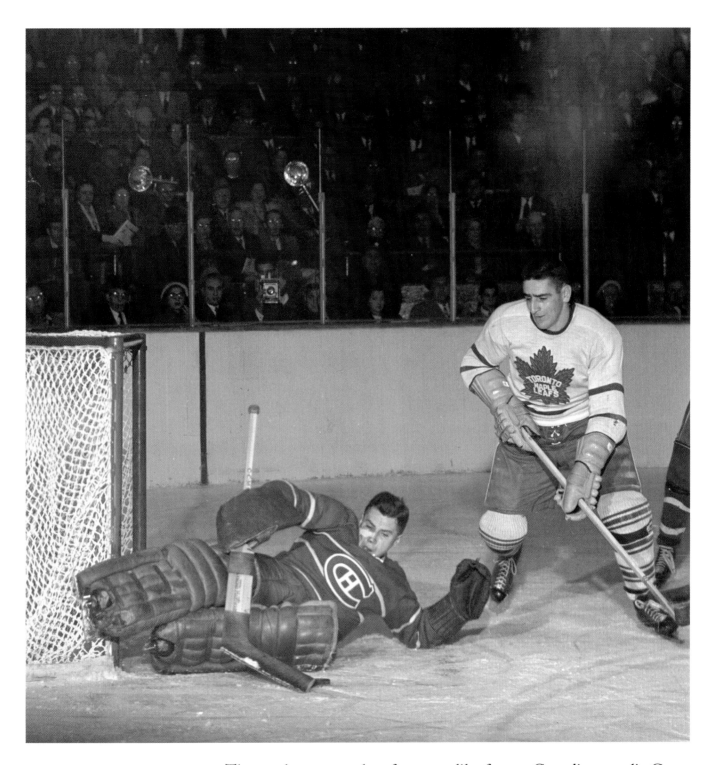

The mask came too late for some, like former Canadiens goalie Gerry McNeil, who lost his nerve and then his job to Jacques Plante in 1954. With Plante hurt in 1956–57, McNeil replaced him for what would be his nine final NHL games. In 1960, as a member of the AHL's Quebec Aces, his final year of pro hockey, he wore a Burchmore-made mask.

There were, however, still many resisters, including some other NHL goalies. One of the most vocal was, again, Gump Worsley. "Why all of a sudden after all these years do they decide we should wear masks?" he asked in 1960. Much of it today sounds like whistling in the dark, or false bravado, but "The Gumper," who played 854 of his 860 NHL games without a mask, liked to say "My face is my mask." He also joked about how unfair it would have been to deprive hockey fans of his "beautiful face."

Leafs legend Johnny Bower remained maskless until the 1968–69 season, finally donning one for the final 18 games of his career. Same for Chicago goalie Glenn Hall, who told sportswriter Jim Hunt, "I know I'm living on borrowed time. But I've been playing without

Johnny Bower of the Toronto Maple Leafs (above) feared his bravery would be questioned if he wore a mask.

Rangers' goalie Gump Worsley (opposite) joked that a mask would deprive fans of seeing his "beautiful face." Worsley was at the other end of the rink on November 1, 1959, when Montreal's Jacques Plante first wore his goalie mask.

one for too long to try one now." Like Bower, Hall would finally adopt one at age 37, in his 15th NHL season.

PLANTE PERSEVERES

While the reception it received wasn't exactly warm, the mask might not have caught on at all had Jacques Plante not won hockey games while wearing one. But win he did, and that, more than anything, made the mask OK with hockey's boss men. After debuting the mask, Plante and the Canadiens went undefeated for 18 consecutive games, a streak that included 10 consecutive wins.

"I had to show good results to keep the mask," Plante would say later. But even though he did, Plante still had to put up with teammates, reporters and fans who suggested he was a coward.

Chicago goaltending great Glenn Hall knew he was "living on borrowed time," but felt he had played without a mask for too long to ever wear one. He changed his mind a few years later.

Jacques Plante (opposite), meanwhile, put together a long winning streak playing behind his new mask.

"Doesn't wearing a mask prove you're scared?" a fan asked him not long after he started wearing one. "If you jumped out of a plane without a parachute," Plante shot back, "would that prove you're brave?"

While Plante was busy trying to win a fifth consecutive Stanley Cup with the Canadiens, Bill Burchmore was back in his workshop. Busy making masks similar to the one he made for Plante, he was also experimenting with ways of improving his basic design. By January of 1960, he had come up with a better, but even weirder looking mask. Rather than using solid sheets of woven fiberglass cloth, Burchmore used 540 ends of fiberglass yarn. The mask actually consisted of fiberglass bars contoured to the face. Almost four ounces lighter and much cooler than the original mask thanks to improved air flow, the design became known as a "pretzel mask" for reasons obvious to anyone who has ever seen one. With its twisted bars and rich caramel color, the mask looks like an extra large version of that salt-speckled, doughy ballpark favorite.

Jacques Plante and Canadiens coach Hector "Toe" Blake feuded over the goalie's mask. Although it is widely believed that Plante never played without a mask again after first wearing one in November 1959, Blake convinced him to go maskless one more time in March 1960.

Jacques Plante (above) wore his first mask for only two months. In January 1960, he wore another Bill Burchmore creation, the so-called "pretzel" mask, which mask maker Greg Harrison would later describe as looking like worms crawling on a goalie's face.

Even with this new and improved version, the effectiveness of the mask was continually questioned that first season. When Plante and the Canadiens hit a rough patch near its end, Toe Blake convinced his goaltender to ditch the mask for a March 8 contest against the Detroit Red Wings. The Canadiens lost the game 3–0 and the mask returned the following night—this time for good. On April 14, the Canadiens beat the Toronto Maple Leafs 4–0 to win their fifth consecutive Stanley Cup, a record that still stands, in a four-game series sweep. Plante posted a 1.38 GAA and earned three shutouts in 14 playoff games that year, and won his fifth straight Vezina Trophy as the NHL's top goaltender.

The Canadiens failed in their bid to win a sixth straight Cup in 1960–61, with Plante having only an average season. Wearing a bigger version of the pretzel mask, another Burchmore innovation, Plante bounced back in 1961–62, a season in which he played in all 70 of his team's games. Even though the league-leading Canadiens were upset by Chicago in the

semi-finals, Plante was named the NHL's Most Valuable Player, the first goaltender ever to receive that honor. He also won the Vezina Trophy with a 2.37 GAA. Other goalies, like Charlie Hodge, who played most of the Canadiens games following Plante's 1963 trade to the New York Rangers, were soon wearing a Burchmore-made pretzel mask.

When Plante first retired in 1965, he actually started a small business venture selling mass-produced pretzel masks called Sunrez Co. Ltd. The masks tended to fit badly, were uncomfortable and difficult to see out of. Made with too much resin, they would also chip in cold arenas. The masks were strong enough, but in their attempt to produce a one-size-fits-all mask, the manufacturers managed to make a "one size fits none."

His pioneering mask efforts aside, Plante's play between the pipes was good enough to earn him the Hart Trophy (above) as the NHL's MVP for the 1961–62 season.

Bill Burchmore made pretzel masks for a number of Montreal junior and pro goaltenders in the early 1960s. The Canadiens' Charlie Hodge (right) wore one painted white.

This mask, however, was an important first step in the development of mass-produced fiberglass masks, especially in terms of a generic fit. Six years later, Plante would return to the business of making and selling masks, this time with more success.

THE SAWCHUK EFFECT

In 1962, another big-name NHL goaltender started wearing a mask. Detroit General Manager Jack Adams, tired of seeing star goalie Terry Sawchuk helped from the ice by trainer Ross "Lefty" Wilson (see *Accidental Mask Maker*, page 59), ordered Wilson to make Sawchuk a mask. Adams was on edge when it came to the health of his goaltenders. In a minor league game in November 1961, Wings prospect Dennis Riggin (the father of NHL goalie Pat Riggin) suffered an eye injury that would eventually end his career. He soldiered on for a while after the injury, and photos exist of him wearing a Louch shield. He actually wore a Lefty Wilson mask in a game before Sawchuk did.

An eye injury to minor league goaltender Dennis Riggin (above, left) caused much consternation in the Detroit Red Wings organization. The team asked trainer Ross "Lefty" Wilson (above, right) to come up with a mask for its goaltenders. The mask he made came to be known as the Sawchuk mask for the goalie who made it famous, even though Dennis Riggin started wearing one before him.

The Lefty Wilson–made mask (right) worn by the legendary Terry Sawchuk from 1962 to 1970.

For Sawchuk, Wilson crafted a rather crude-looking, basic mask from five sheets of fiberglass and cut large eyeholes in it. The inverted "T" running from the nose to the mouth, as well as three tiny ventilation holes on the sides of the nose, gave the mask a cat-like appearance. But the masks were light and comfortable and the large eyeholes made following the puck easy.

It was another breakthrough for the mask. Oddball Jacques Plante wearing a mask was one thing, but once the great Sawchuk started wearing one, the hockey establishment finally started to truly embrace it.

"It wasn't until Sawchuk put on the mask that the Canadiens really accepted it," a bitter-sounding Plante told sportswriter Jim Hunt in 1967. "He was one of the game's superstars and if he wore one it had to be all right."

Sawchuk wore the mask sporadically at first as it took some getting used to. But by October of 1962 he was wearing it regularly. In an October 31st article in the *Detroit News* newspaper, Sawchuk joked of wearing his mask to scare trick-or-treaters that night. Two months later, he told the same newspaper that he felt more confident and alert wearing his mask, claiming that its blind spots kept him on his toes more.

While playing for the Los Angeles Kings in 1968, Sawchuk was hit under the right eye by a slapshot off the stick of Chicago's Pit Martin. The force of the shot cracked Sawchuk's mask and cut his cheekbone. Kings trainer (and practice goalie) Danny Wood attempted to repair the cracked mask, even though Sawchuk had

LEFTY WILSON: Accidental Mask Maker

Ross "Lefty" Wilson was a hockey legend in his own right, not because of his skills as a goaltender but as the colorful, outspoken trainer of the Detroit Red Wings from 1950 to 1982. In the 1950s, the trainer on a hockey team had to be a jack-of-all-trades: he was responsible for everything from stitching equipment (and faces), to being a practice and emergency backup for both teams during home games in the days when teams only carried one goalie. Wilson actually played in three NHL games. In 1953, he played 20 shutout minutes for Detroit, subbing for the legendary Terry Sawchuk. In 1956, he replaced the Leafs' Harry Lumley for 17 minutes of shutout hockey. And in 1958, he played almost an entire game for Boston when Bruins goalie Don Simmons was injured, allowing just one goal against his own Red Wings!

In 1962, Red Wings management instructed Wilson to make a mask for star goalie Terry Sawchuk. He and his partner, fellow trainer Donny Olesevich, taught themselves how to make a face mold and how to work with fiberglass.

They made a crude but functional mask for Sawchuk, who credited the creation with extending his career.

Because of Sawchuk's brilliance when wearing the mask, Wilson's mask-making skills were soon in high demand. Like Bill Burchmore before him, he started receiving orders for masks from all over. With the Red Wings' permission, Wilson made masks for other pro goaltenders, charging only $35 for them. Wilson's masks remained popular with pro goalies throughout the 1960s. Roger Crozier, Roy Edwards, Cesare Maniago and Jim Rutherford all wore a Lefty Wilson mask at some point in their careers. Hall of Famer Gerry Cheevers, who would later make mask history himself, and who broke into the NHL without a mask with the Toronto Maple Leafs during the 1961–62 season, ended up wearing a Lefty Wilson mask with the Boston Bruins in the mid-1960s. Even goalies who went without a mask during games, like Toronto's Johnny Bower and Boston's Bruce Gamble, would wear a Wilson mask in practices.

Lefty Wilson (left) and Donny Olesevich (right)

Terry Sawchuk

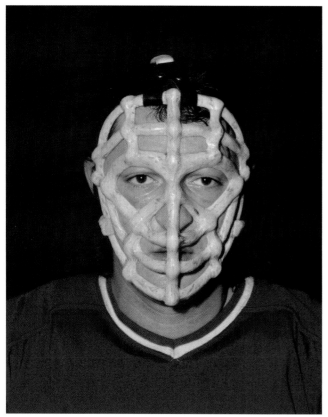

another. Sawchuk always felt most comfortable in his original "Lefty" mask and, like many athletes, superstition prevented him from changing masks. Sawchuk's original Lefty Wilson mask now rests in the Hockey Hall of Fame in Toronto where one can clearly see the repair work under the right eye opening.

New Faces

Bill Burchmore stopped making masks in the late 1960s. Around that same time another mask maker appeared, one who also favored the pretzel design. Halifax native and former Junior A player Roy Weatherbee came up with his own version of the pretzel, one that caught on with young goalies like Boston's Bernie Parent, and, post-1967 expansion, Los Angeles' Jacques Caron and Philadelphia's Dunc Wilson and Doug Favell. Though similar in design and technique to Burchmore's original pretzel, Weatherbee's masks were lighter and stronger thanks to his understanding of the flex and tensile strength of fiberglass.

By the mid-1960s, most of the NHL goalies that had adopted the mask were either wearing pretzel masks or Lefty Wilson designs... with mixed results. Even though they were custom-made, these early masks tended to move on the goalie's face when action heated up around the goalmouth. A plumber from Massachusetts changed all that. After word of a mask he made for his son made its way into the Boston Bruins' dressing room, Ernie Higgins (see *From Plumber to Pioneer,* page 64) of nearby Norwood, Massachusetts, soon had orders from Boston goalies Gerry Cheevers and Eddie Johnston. Higgins' masks were revolutionary and

In the late 1960s and early '70s, Roy Weatherbee's version of the pretzel mask was popular with goaltenders on some of the NHL's newest teams. Clockwise from top left: Philadelphia's Bernie Parent, Jacques Caron of the St. Louis Blues, Philadelphia's Doug Favell and Vancouver's Dunc Wilson.

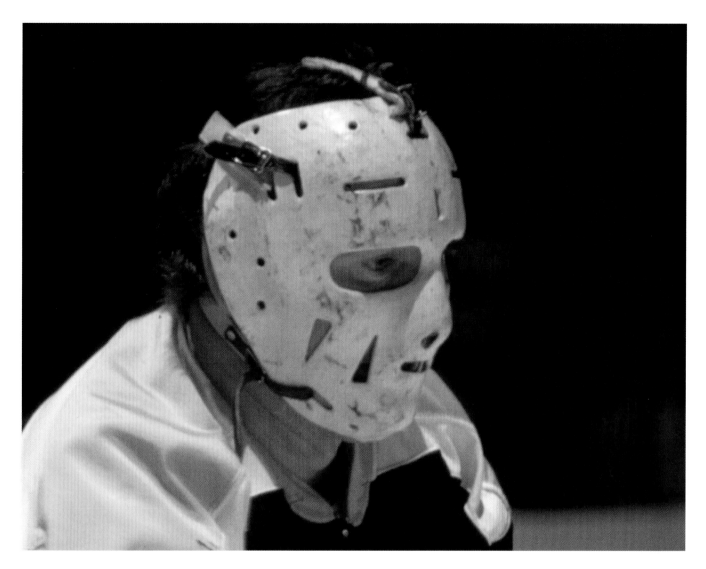

instantly recognizable by their shape and many ventilation holes and slits. They were bigger, offering more protection, but fit better too. They also moved around less, thanks to a rounded chin that more or less anchored the mask to the goaltender's face. By the beginning of the 1970s, Higgins' masks were the most widely used in the NHL, and remained the dominant mask type for much of the next decade.

An Expansion in Mask Making

By the time the NHL added six teams in 1967, it was the maskless goalie that had become the oddity. Among the holdouts were old-timers Johnny Bower, Glenn Hall and Gump Worsley, as well as Ed Giacomin, who debuted with the New York Rangers in 1965 but didn't start wearing a

Rangers goalie Ed Giacomin (opposite) played five NHL seasons without a mask before being fitted for an Ernie Higgins model in 1970. Boston Bruins goalie Eddie Johnston (above), also one of the last maskless goalies in the NHL, was one of Higgins' first NHL customers.

ERNIE HIGGINS: From Plumber to Pioneer

Hockey's most important mask maker for the better part of a decade actually came to the game via his goaltending son. A future NCAA netminder at Boston College, Neil Higgins was still a youth hockey goalie when he complained about his ill-fitting and expensive store-bought goalie mask to his father, Norwood, Massachusetts, plumbing supervisor Ernie Higgins. In 1962, in his basement workshop, Higgins senior set about making his son a mask of his own, one that fit. Within a few years, he had perfected a mask-making technique and design that saw the best goaltenders in the world heading down his basement steps to be fitted for an Ernie Higgins model of their own.

In 1967, after Neil Higgins met former Bruins netminder Ed Chadwick at a summer hockey school, word of Higgins' mask work made its way into the home team's dressing room at the nearby Boston Garden. Higgins was invited to meet Bruins goalies Eddie Johnston and Gerry Cheevers, the latter unsatisfied with the Lefty Wilson model he was using. Cheevers felt that the greatest flaw of the relatively flat masks most goalies used at that time were that they moved, so Higgins set about designing a rounder mask, one that curved under the chin and held fast. The Higgins model, instantly recognizable by the ventilation slits (or holes in later models) in a "T" formation across the forehead and triangular ventilation slots on the cheeks, was soon the most used mask in hockey, worn by top goaltenders

In this 1968 **Boston Globe** *photo,*
Ernie Higgins puts the finishing touches
on a mask for Bruins goalie Eddie Johnston.

like Cheevers, Ed Giacomin, Rogie Vachon, Doug Favell and countless other pro and amateur goalies in the late1960s and '70s.

By 1969 Higgins was the first ever full-time maker of goalie masks. Later, he made and designed pros-thetic devices and special casts for injured athletes and accident victims, including a lightweight, removable one for the leg of Boston Red Sox slugger Ken Harrelson. Over the years, Higgins continued to improve his design, adding a back plate and, after Eddie Johnston was struck by a shot in the side of the head, extending the mask over and around the sides of the goaltender's head. By the mid-1970s, the full-head Higgins mask, worn by Favell and Gary Smith, was for all intents and purposes a complete helmet, the precursor of today's masks.

Ernie Higgins took safety seriously, and regularly consulted with engineers and doctors on his mask designs. He was also known to give masks away to young goalies who could not afford one. Higgins took great pride in his work. According to one story, whenever he heard that a goaltender was injured wearing one of his creations—a rare event—Higgins was moved to tears.

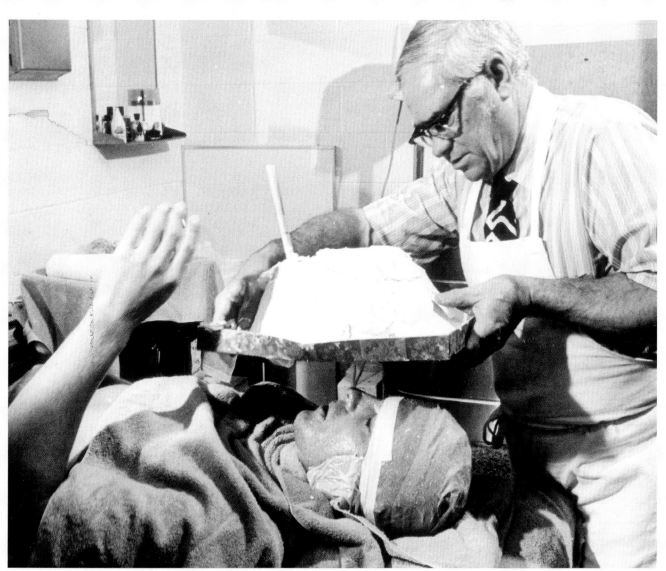

Ernie Higgins removes a plaster mold from the face of an unknown goaltender in 1978. In the 1960s and '70s, many of the NHL's top netminders made a trip to Higgins' Norwood, Massachusetts, home to be fitted for a new mask.

Even though he could have turned
to one of the growing number
of mask makers, Chicago's Dave
Dryden (right) continued to wear
a mask he made himself in 1962.

Rogie Vachon's first mask (left) was
made by Tom Lawson, a trainer on
one of the Montreal Canadiens
farm teams. Vachon, who debuted
in the NHL without a mask in
1966–67, started wearing one in
the late 1960s and kept it after
he was traded to the Los Angeles
Kings in 1971. He switched to an
Ernie Higgins model shortly after.

mask until 1970. The mask he finally adopted was an Ernie Higgins model. Giacomin wore his Higgins mask until he was traded to the Red Wings in 1976. Giacomin liked teammate Jim Rutherford's Greg Harrison-made mask and ordered one like it for himself. Ironically, Harrison's first NHL client was Rutherford who had asked the young mask maker to design a mask like Giacomin's Higgins-style mask.

With more NHL and minor league teams, and at least two goaltenders on every one of them, there were more goaltenders than ever before, most of whom wanted a mask. The mask-making business boomed, and a number of new mask makers emerged.

Dave Dryden, brother of Hall of Famer Ken Dryden, was one of the few NHL goalies without a Higgins, Wilson or Weatherbee mask. He made his own mask in 1962 and used it in his NHL debut with the Chicago Blackhawks in 1965. He made a second mask in 1970 and was wearing it the night he faced his brother in a historic 1971 matchup as a member of the Buffalo Sabres.

Like Lefty Wilson before him, another trainer turned mask maker was Tom Lawson, an expert skate sharpener who worked in the Montreal Canadiens farm system in the late 1950s and early '60s. Lawson later worked for the Hull-Ottawa Canadiens, a farm team in the old Eastern Professional Hockey League, where he crossed paths with some of the goalies he later made masks for, including Montreal netminders Charlie

Seth Martin (above) made his mark backstopping Canadian amateur teams in international play in the 1950s and '60s. He also made masks for himself and other amateur goaltenders, including some in Europe.

Jacques Plante replaced Seth Martin in the St. Louis Blues net in 1968–69. The two mask pioneers seem to have made an impression on their teammate, the great Glenn Hall (facing page), who started wearing a Martin-made mask after going maskless for 15 NHL seasons.

FOLLOWING PAGES:

Jacques Plante came out of retirement to join the St. Louis Blues for the 1968–69 season wearing the second of his Bill Burchmore-made pretzel masks.

Jacques Plante was wearing this mask, one he designed with Montrealer David Britt, when he was knocked unconscious by a Fred Stanfield shot during the 1970 playoffs. The small fracture the mask sustained can be seen over its left eyehole.

Hodge, Rogie Vachon, Phil Myre and Ernie Wakely. Lawson's masks were unique, with large eye openings and ventilation holes across the forehead that looked like a picket fence.

The great Glenn Hall was the first of the old guard to cave in and wear a mask, one year after the St. Louis Blues plucked him from the Chicago Blackhawks in the 1967 expansion draft.

"I want to be sure I can collect my paycheck personally from now on," Hall told sports reporters inquiring about his new look. "I don't want it mailed to the Good Samaritan Hospital... or cemetery."

His backup that year was Seth Martin, a British Columbia native well known overseas for having defended the nets of various teams representing Canada in international events.

While Johnny Bower will forever be remembered as going bare-faced in goal, he actually wore a mask created by a dentist friend in 1968–69, his final full NHL season.

In 1960, Martin was playing in the Allan Cup playoffs when he was hit in the mouth with a shot that cut him open for stitches. The injury convinced Martin to try playing with a mask. But since he didn't know where he could get one, Martin decided to make his own. He had the team physician make a mold of his face and then went to a local fiberglass shop to learn how to work with mask-making materials. The next season, Martin led the Trail Smoke Eaters to a World Championship while wearing his homemade mask. He went on to make masks for many Western circuit senior goalies in the early 1960s. When he joined the Canadian National Team in 1963, Martin became one of the first goalies to wear a fiberglass mask in international play. In fact, Martin was responsible for the mask's migration across the Atlantic, having made masks for goalies in Sweden and other European countries. Soviet hockey officials even lowered the Iron Curtain to allow Martin to make masks for Russian and Czechoslovakian goalies.

Tony Esposito wore a Jacques Plante and David Britt mask from 1969 until he retired in 1984. He had it modified for better safety in the 1970s and '80s.

Johnny Bower had worn masks in practice as early as the mid-1950s, including a Louch shield and fiberglass masks made by both Lefty Wilson and Ernie Higgins. But he never felt comfortable with any of them, and when he finally adopted a mask in the fall of 1968, his final season, it was one made by his neighbor, a dentist by the name of Dr. Rick Bell. Bower has said that his large nose blocked his vision in his other molded masks, but that the one made by Dr. Bell had fewer blind spots. Bell died in a 1967 car accident, shortly after completing Bower's mask.

PLANTE RETURNS TO THE NHL… AND MASK MAKING

Meanwhile, Jacques Plante came out of retirement to join his old rival Glenn Hall with the St. Louis Blues in 1968, wearing the second of his pretzel masks made by Bill Burchmore. In 1969, he debuted another mask, a more solid white model he developed in collaboration with Montrealer David Britt. A former goalie, Britt worked in the airline industry and was familiar with the new generation of resins and cloths developed for it. He and Plante formed an unusual partnership: They would sketch out mask designs on napkins in airport waiting areas and then bring them to mask makers. Britt also hooked up with other NHL goalies in airports, convincing them to try the new design. And because Plante was busy stopping pucks for the Blues, it was Britt who would take the mold impression of goalies' faces and deliver the final product to them at the Montreal Forum.

The Plante-Britt masks were models of durability. Chicago's Tony Esposito wore the same one for 15 years with the Blackhawks. Plante and Britt also designed masks for NHL goalies like Denis Dejordy, Al Smith, Les Binkley and Ernie Wakely. Plante was wearing this mask when he was knocked unconscious by a Fred Stanfield slapshot during a

FOLLOWING PAGES
Bernie Parent was a Jacques Plante disciple in every way. He wore a Fibrosport mask for most of the 1970s.

Jacques Plante poses proudly with his Fibrosport mask for his last hockey card photo. He ended his second retirement to play goal for the Edmonton Oilers of the WHA in 1974–75, and retired for good at the end of that season at the age of 45.

JACQUES PLANTE: The Fibrosport Venture

Jacques Plante's second stab at manufacturing and selling goalie masks commercially resulted in the founding of an enterprise called Fibrosport, of which Plante himself was president. Formed in Magog, Quebec, in 1970, the company sold both custom-made and mass-produced masks based on the one he helped develop after his injury in the 1970 playoffs.

Made of high-impact fiberglass and epoxy resin, and featuring ridges that would deflect pucks away instead of absorbing the full impact, Fibrosport masks were considered to be the best masks ever made, at least according to Plante, and he marketed them aggressively. Mass-produced Fibrosport masks retailed for $12 to $18, while a custom- made pro model similar to what Plante wore at the end of his NHL career sold for $150 in 1971.

Among the goalies to wear the Fibrosport mask at some point in their careers were Plante himself, Bruce Gamble, Bernie Parent, Phil Myre, Roger Crozier, Michel Plasse, Ron Low, Gary Edwards and Gilles Gilbert. Flyers' great Pelle Lindbergh's first mask was a Fibrosport.

At its peak, Fibrosport produced upwards of 8,000 masks per year, and boasted worldwide sales. The business ceased operating in 1979, a victim of the popularity of cages and new rules about mask use for amateur players.

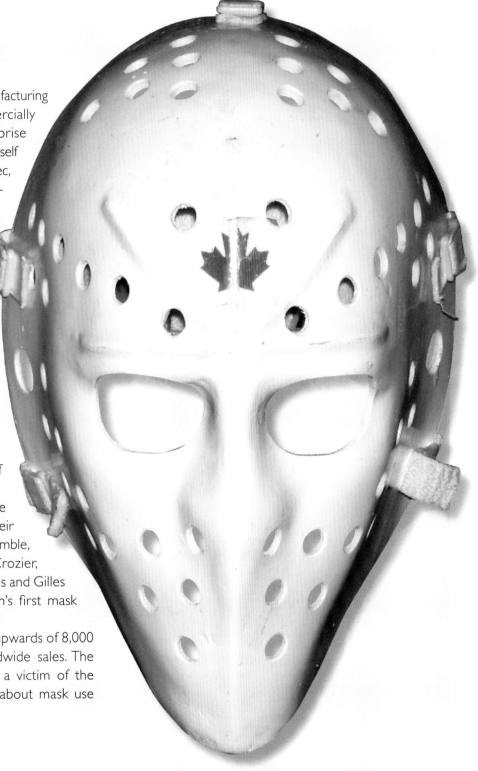

1970 playoff game against the Boston Bruins. The shot was so hard that it fractured the mask. This led Plante to develop a new mask, made by his new company, Fibrosport (see *The Fibrosport Venture,* page 75), later that year. The game against Boston ended up being Plante's last one with the Blues; he would be a Toronto Maple Leaf for the next three seasons.

The identity of those who physically made the masks Plante designed with David Britt is not known. Over the years, Plante had developed a large network of friends, some of them Fibreglass Canada employees, who experimented with mask making. Some would later come to work for him at Fibrosport.

At Fibrosport, Plante and his team of designers quickly developed a ridged mask able to withstand the force of pucks fired at 135 mph. Prior to the 1970–71 season, Plante demonstrated the new mask at the NHL's summer meetings and went on to wear one for parts of three seasons in Toronto, eight games in Boston, and, later, after ending his second and even shorter retirement, with the Edmonton Oilers of the World Hockey Association in 1974–75. It became the Fibrosport mask.

Plante was convinced that Fibrosport masks were the best made and began to aggressively pursue his fellow goalies to convince them to try them. Although they never quite challenged the Ernie Higgins masks as the dominant mask style in the NHL, the Fibrosport models were worn by a number of goalies for many years. Hall of Famer Bernie Parent, a Jacques Plante disciple if ever there was one, wore a Fibrosport mask from 1970 until his injury-forced retirement in 1979.

Ken Dryden and his Bill Burchmore-made mask debuted in the NHL in 1971. Dryden had the mask as early as the mid-1960s, wearing it between the pipes at Cornell University.

One of hockey's most unusual masks, worn by one of its most unusual goaltenders, Hall of Famer Ken Dryden, debuted in 1971. The mask itself, however, was several years old by then. Part standard mask and part pretzel type, the mask was actually worn by Dryden for several years at Cornell University before he broke in with the Montreal Canadiens. All goalies in U.S. college hockey were required to wear facial protection, so Dryden had a mold made in Toronto and sent it to Montreal, presumably to Bill Burchmore. (Burchmore's son claims that his father made the mask.) Dryden himself does not remember the origins of the mask. By the time Dryden made it to the NHL, the mask was falling apart. Chipped and worn, some of its bars were held together by hockey tape.

JIM HOMUTH: Mask Perfectionist

Like many mask makers, Jim Homuth was a goaltender who started making his own masks out of necessity. In 1969, the Ottawa firefighter decided to create his own facial protection after suffering a few lacerations in games. He tried a few different masks but felt the fit and vision were inadequate. After watching Jacques Plante collapse to the ice after taking a Fred Stanfield slapshot off the forehead in the Stanley Cup playoffs, Homuth felt that he could make a safer mask. Homuth was a perfectionist who went about making his masks in a scientific way; experimenting and testing, often having shooters fire pucks at his own head. He studied the tensile strength of fiberglass and experimented until he arrived at what he felt was the perfect mask. Homuth used a special mixture of resins and fiberglass, reinforcing, spending countless hours studying their properties, and testing, until he arrived at what he felt was the best formula and design. Once this was determined, he never deviated, making all his masks exactly the same way. Homuth, along with Plante, was instrumental in advancing the design of the mask by adding forehead ridges and a pointed, angled nose area that ran down to the chin, ensuring there were no flat spots and that a puck would glance off the goalie's head upon impact.

Homuth made his first NHL mask for Gary Smith in 1972, and, through word of mouth, several other

Veteran Phil Myre wore a Jim Homuth-made mask as a member of the Atlanta Flames.

pro and junior goalies were soon asking him to make masks for them. His clients included Ken Dryden, Joe Daley, Michel Plasse, Gilles Gratton, Phil Myre, Dan Bouchard, Billy Smith and Gerry Desjardins. Although his masks were well regarded and in demand, Homuth took his time making them, producing only 10 to 15 per year and only in spring and summer. He made about 75 masks in total for pro, junior and college goalies.

Ken Dryden's first mask was a modified pretzel made by Bill Burchmore around 1964. Dryden wore the mask until he had a new one made by Jim Homuth in 1976.

Dryden wore the mask until 1973. He missed the 1973–74 season due to a contract dispute, and returned the following year with a mask made by Jim Homuth, an Ottawa firefighter and another ex-goaltender who started making masks out of necessity (see *Mask Perfectionist*, above). Together with Ernie Higgins and Jacques Plante's Fibrosport, he would help supply masks for many NHL goalies throughout the 1970s.

By 1972, only a few maskless diehards remained. That year, North American hockey fans got their first look at something followers of international hockey had known about for many years—a mask that didn't fit

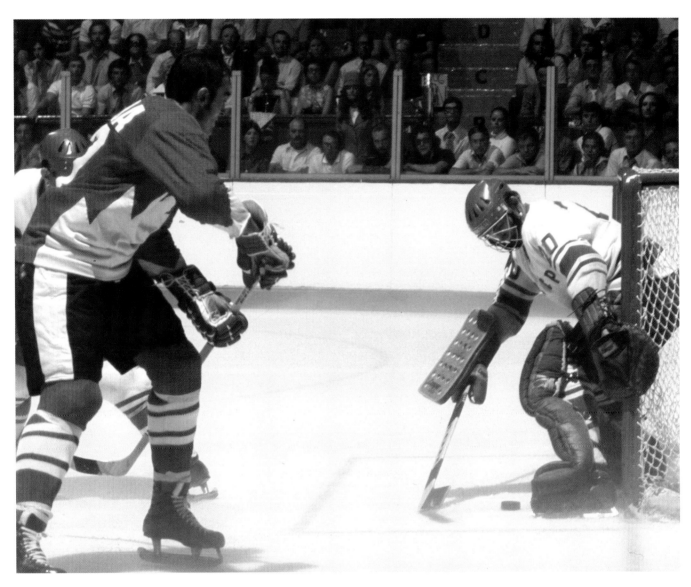

flush against the face, and that didn't require the wearer to sit through a face mold torture session. In the famous Summit Series, considered by many to be the finest hockey ever played, a powerful team from the then Union of Soviet Socialist Republics (USSR) came to Canada to take on a team made up of the NHL's finest, including goaltenders Tony Esposito and Ken Dryden. The Soviets were led by their goaltender, the now legendary Vladislav Tretiak, who wore not a fiberglass mask, but a flimsy plastic helmet fitted with a wire "birdcage." Tretiak's mask-cage combo seemed an oddity at the time, but it would contribute to the transformation of the mask in less than a decade. The fiberglass goalie mask was about to receive its first real challenge.

USSR goalie Vladislav Tretiak makes a save on Team Canada's Frank Mahovlich during the legendary Summit Series in 1972.

Behind bars: The first birdcage mask most North American hockey fans ever saw was the one worn by Vladislav Tretiak of the USSR during the 1972 Summit Series. But the birdcage didn't show up in the NHL until 1976.

Chapter Three

PAINT JOBS AND
METAL BARS

By 1970, there were goalie masks of all types, made by several different mask makers and even mask companies such as Jacques Plante's Fibrosport. What these different masks had in common was their color, or rather their lack of it. Although a few of the older masks were still the dark, natural hue of the fiberglass they were made from, most masks were painted white... just white.

A goalie who hated white changed all that by drawing ugly little black marks all over a mask made by a man who loved white. With a few strokes of his black marker, Boston's Gerry Cheevers unknowingly started a seemingly irreversible trend, decorating or personalizing the goalie mask. Soon, there were different colored paints, then some simple graphics and, within a few years, goalie masks were completely transformed from plain pieces of protective equipment to colorful works of art.

There were other big changes for the goalie mask in the 1970s. The so-called birdcage mask (or cage-helmet combo as it is also known) became the mask of choice for goaltenders of all ages, especially after a couple of high-profile eye injuries suffered by goalies wearing molded masks. Thanks to the ingenuity of a veteran goalie, and arguably the greatest mask maker that hockey has ever known, the best qualities of both types of masks were soon combined to create the safest mask yet.

Gerry Cheevers' stitches mask was simple and clever in its design, and remains the most recognizable mask in the history of hockey.

Mask maker Ernie Higgins liked things white. His masks were white, and just about everything in the basement workshop where he crafted them was white, too. Higgins even dressed all in white as he slathered white plaster over the faces of the goalies who came to him for masks. So he couldn't have been too pleased to see what Boston Bruins goalie Gerry Cheevers, his first big league customer, did to his mask in the late 1960s.

Cheevers was no fan of white. He felt it represented purity, which was not exactly the way he saw himself... or the way he played goal, for that matter. Cheevers often recounts how he created the single most recognizable mask of all time. Basically, after taking a shot off his mask in practice one day, a blow he later said "wouldn't have hurt a canary," the colorful Cheevers, notorious for his dislike of practicing, retreated to the dressing room. Some stories have him drinking a beer and smoking a cigarette when Bruins coach Harry Sinden finally tracked him down, but he was more likely sipping on a Coke when the coach chased him back out onto the ice. When Cheevers returned to his net, his mask sported a huge black stitch mark where the puck had struck the mask, crudely drawn by Bruins trainer John "Frosty" Forristall at Cheevers' request. Soon, it was Cheevers' teammates who were in stitches.

The story is true... except it wasn't the first time Cheevers had added stitch marks to one of his masks. The St. Catharines, Ontario, native actually made his NHL debut with the Toronto Maple Leafs in 1962 and played two games without a mask. When he finally returned to the big leagues with the Bruins in 1966, Cheevers was still maskless. Not long after, though, he started wearing a Lefty Wilson-made, "Sawchuk style" mask, one that can be seen in photos with several black stitch marks and

Gerry Cheevers wore an Ernie Higgins mask, which he famously covered with faux stitch marks, from 1967 until his retirement in 1980. But he also decorated his first ever mask, a Lefty Wilson creation, with a few stitch marks in 1966–67.

a long red one over its left eye. So Cheevers had tried the stitches gag at least once before he added a little color to his Higgins mask.

Regardless, the stitches were a hit with Cheevers' teammates, fans and the media, and Cheevers continued to add stitches to his mask every time a puck struck it. By the time he retired the mask in 1980, it was virtually covered with stitch marks, which is probably not too great an exaggeration considering what the faces of some pre-mask goalies looked like at the end of their careers. Cheevers later said that he would receive letters from fans young and old asking how they too could get such a neat mask. "Send me $100," Cheevers would reply, "and I'll send you a Magic Marker."

MASKS OF A DIFFERENT COLOR

Although Doug Favell of the Philadelphia Flyers is widely credited with introducing the painted mask to the NHL during the 1971–72 season, much-traveled goaltender Gary Smith actually beat him to it a

few months earlier. Smith, who earned the nickname "Suitcase" early in his career, played for eight different NHL teams and one World Hockey Association team between 1965 and 1980. He was a member of the Oakland Seals when the team was sold and became the California Golden Seals before the 1970–71 season. The team's new owner was Charles O. Finley, who also owned Major League Baseball's Oakland Athletics. The colorful Finley brought a number of "innovations" to the game, including white skates and later skates in the team's colors. Whether it was Finley's or Smith's idea is not known, but Gary Smith had his Ernie Higgins-made mask painted yellow to match the team's yellow and green uniforms sometime that season.

In a case of yet more twisted mask lore, Doug Favell brought some additional color to the game the following season. Some stories say he was the victim of a prank, while others say he asked the trainers on the Philadelphia Flyers to do it for him. But regardless of whose idea

The Red Wings'
Jim Rutherford would
eventually have
team logos added
above the eyeholes
of his mask.

it was, Favell's Ernie Higgins mask was painted a jarring Halloween orange before an October 31 game against the Los Angeles Kings. "Favy," as he was known to his teammates, soon had a new nickname: "The Great Pumpkin." Later, Favell and the Flyers' backup goalie, Bobby Taylor, each had a striped sunburst design painted on their masks. Favell sported orange stripes, while Taylor, who claims his came first, had black stripes on his mask.

Around the same time Doug Favell was sporting his new pumpkin look, Detroit trainer Lefty Wilson was painting Red Wings rookie netminder Jim Rutherford's mask red. Rutherford actually made his NHL debut in 1970–71 without a mask, but then took to wearing a Wilson model—one that would be painted red at some point that season. How many times he wore it is unknown, but the mask appears in Esso NHL Power Players, a 1970–71 promotion in which collectible stickers were given out with a purchase of gasoline.

Rutherford's early career kept mask makers and painters alike busy. His Wilson mask had to be painted white again when he was picked up in an inter-league draft by the Pittsburgh Penguins in 1971–72. In 1973, Rutherford met an amateur goalie and art student by the name of Greg Harrison (see *Mask Maestro*, page 102) at a hockey school. Harrison was also a budding mask maker, designing masks similar in style to those made by Ernie Higgins. Rutherford ordered a mask, and had Harrison paint it Penguins blue. It was the first NHL mask for Harrison, who would go on to make hundreds and become the greatest goalie mask maker ever.

After two and a half seasons with Pittsburgh, Rutherford was traded back to Detroit in January 1974, which meant the powder blue just wouldn't do. Luckily for Rutherford, Detroit's next game was in Toronto, where Harrison lived. Rutherford asked Harrison to paint his mask white, but the young mask maker couldn't help himself and painted a red wing over each eye of the mask, the eyeholes completing the winged wheel logo of the Red Wings.

"I wasn't looking at starting a new fad or make a fashion statement," Rutherford told *USA Today* in 2007. "At the morning skate, [Harrison] comes in with a big smile on, and [the mask] had wings on it. I was upset. I didn't like it, but I had no other choice except to wear it."

The mask was so popular with fans that Rutherford felt obliged to keep it. Even though he changed masks at least once in between, he kept the same wings design until he was traded to Toronto in 1980.

Rogie Vachon of the Los Angeles Kings gave his Ernie Higgins-made mask a unique look in the early 1970s, but it had nothing to do with paint. For some reason, he had the mouth opening cut to resemble a smile.

Fans got a charge out of the electrical sparks painted on Ed Giacomin's mask.

"The Gumper" is shown in one of the 855 games he played bare-faced (left), and one of only six in which he was masked (right).

A few years later, he had a purple paint job done on another Higgins mask, complete with a pair of Kings' crown logos over the eyes.

Hell froze over in the spring of 1974—sort of. That year, after 25 professional seasons and 855 games played without a mask, Lorne "Gump" Worsley, the biggest mask detractor of all time, played the final six games of his career with a mask. He conceded to wear it after friends and family begged him to do so. At the age of 44, Worsley's career was obviously nearing its end. So, after having tempted fate for so long, he and his Minnesota North Stars goaltending partner, Cesare Maniago, visited Minnesota mask maker William Cossette. It was actually Maniago who convinced Worsley that life after hockey would be more enjoyable with both of his eyes. As for the mask itself, Worsley, true to form, hated it to the bitter end. He said it was too warm, and flipped it up on his head whenever the puck was at the opposite end of the rink.

Many hockey fans still believe Worsley to be the last NHL goalie to go maskless, and some newspaper obituaries published after his passing in January 2007 actually said he was. But that honor goes to Andy Brown, a backup goalie on the Pittsburgh Penguins in 1974 (see *The Last Brave Face*, page 94).

While with Los Angeles, Rogie Vachon had a smile added to the mouth opening of his deep purple mask, and crowns above the eye openings to reflect the team's royal name.

Doug Favell chose to honor the Leafs with a single blue one.

DESIGNER MASKS

While Rutherford was making waves with his red wings, other goalies were busy adding color and logos to their masks, too. Bernie Parent had a flame motif painted on the mask he wore with the WHA's Philadelphia Blazers in 1972–73, and added a Flyers logo to a white Fibrosport mask when he returned to the NHL the following season. When Doug Favell was traded to Toronto in 1973, he had a large blue maple leaf painted on the forehead of a white Ernie Higgins mask. Greg Harrison made Favell's next mask, which had an even larger leaf across the face.

Former Rangers great Ed Giacomin had Greg Harrison make him a new mask when he joined the Detroit Red Wings in 1975. The mask had electrical sparks painted across the top in what some said was part of a possible endorsement deal with a sparkplug company. Legend has it that the NHL disallowed the endorsement. Regardless of whether that is true or not, the mask, with Giacomin's silver hair sprouting out the sides and top of it, gave the future Hall of Famer a look all his own.

A few years later, Harrison made a mask for Toronto goalie Wayne Thomas which featured a series of white maple leaves painted on a large

THE LAST BRAVE FACE: Andy Brown

Lorne "Gump" Worsley was easily the most stubborn goaltender of all time, playing all but the last six of his 861 career NHL games without a mask. Many hockey fans mistakenly believe "The Gumper" to be the last goalie to play in an NHL game without facial protection, but that feat was performed by the perhaps equally hard-headed but little-known Andy Brown, a journeyman backup goalie who played in only 62 NHL games with Detroit and Pittsburgh. On April 7, 1974, in a 6–3 Penguins loss to the Atlanta Flames, the Hamilton, Ontario-born Brown defended his team's net bare-faced. It was the end of an era for hockey, and Brown too, for the game ended up being his last in the NHL. By 1975, every NHL goalie was wearing a mask. During that 1974 NHL season, Brown did in fact wear a mask during practices, but felt it hindered his vision in games. Brown continued to play in the WHA... without a mask.

blue X. The mask, which featured a sleeker look than the ones he'd made previously, was Harrison's first original design.

In 1976, Montreal's Ken Dryden debuted a new mask made by Jim Homuth. Dryden loved the way the mask fit, but he and Homuth locked horns over some changes the future Hall of Famer and Liberal Member of Parliament wanted made. Dryden asked for more ventilation and bigger eye openings, but Homuth refused to modify the mask for fear of compromising its strength. So Dryden took the mask to a sports equipment designer named Carl Lamb, who cut larger eye openings, filled in Homuth's small circular ventilation holes and created larger, triangular ones. Lamb also painted a simple design on the mask: a red circle in the shape of the Canadiens' crest inside a larger blue one. On a white background, the circles provided a target effect. Yes, dark goalie humor was alive and well.

Tempting fate: Ken Dryden's Jim Homuth-made, Carl Lamb-designed mask invited shooters to aim for the bull's-eye.

New York Islanders goaltender Glenn "Chico" Resch can lay claim to the first truly elaborate mask design. In 1976, he let New York art student Linda Spinella, the friend of an Islanders locker room attendant, dress up his Ernie Higgins mask. Spinella painted the mask Islanders blue, and added the team's island logo across the brow and the letters "NY" across the forehead. Although Resch himself wasn't crazy about the new look, and considered the mask too "showy," the design was a hit with fans on the Island. And since he played well while wearing it, Resch decided to keep it.

Other mask designers started painting their creations around the same time. In the mid-'70s, a mask maker named Rob Harris made a new mask for Maple Leafs goaltender Mike Palmateer. It featured a slightly elongated chin for more protection and had broad blue-and-white stripes and blue maple leaves across it. It also displayed one of the first examples of mask personalization, prominently featuring Palmateer's number 29 on one side of the forehead.

The popularity of the first designed masks opened the floodgates of creativity and expression. Soon, just about every goalie wanted a fancy mask paint job. Many of them called upon Greg Harrison, whose reputation as both a designer and mask maker was growing quickly. Among those turning to Harrison for masks with a dash or more of color in the years that followed were Denis Herron of the Kansas City Scouts, John Davidson of the New York Rangers and Vancouver's Curt Ridley, whose mask featured a pair of Canucks stick logos crossed on the face.

Glenn "Chico" Resch's mask while with the New York Islanders is said to have showcased the first elaborate design, including an illustrated Long Island across the brow, and the letters "NY" across the forehead.

As the 1970s progressed, so too did the complexity of mask designs. The one-time California Golden Seals goaltending duo of Gary Simmons and Gilles Meloche wore two of the most popular masks ever. Simmons, who went by the nickname "Cobra," had Greg Harrison paint a coiled green snake rising up on a black mask. The mask proved popular with Golden Seals fans, most of whom didn't notice that the Canadian artist had painted the cobra complete with rattlers—a feature the species does not possess.

When the Golden Seals franchise moved to Cleveland to become the Barons in 1976–77, Gilles Meloche ordered a new mask paint job from Harrison, who created his own Cleveland coat of arms, painted red and white on a black background. The "heraldry" mask, like many Harrison creations, is now prominently featured in the mask display in Toronto's Hockey Hall of Fame.

FIBERGLASS LION

Harrison's most famous mask is arguably the one he made for New York Rangers goaltender Gilles Gratton in 1976. A native of LaSalle, Quebec, Gratton enjoyed some success in Junior hockey and with the Toronto Toros of the WHA. But he will be remembered most for the masks he wore during his only full season in the NHL. In one game, he actually wore a different mask in each period: two "birdcages" and a fiberglass model. Gratton was an oddball who would jump up and down with glee in the dressing room upon hearing that he would not be his team's starting goaltender. He once told a group of Rangers season ticket holders that in a past life he had been a Spanish count who liked to line commoners up

Kansas City's Denis Herron and New York's John Davidson wore popular Greg Harrison designs while with the Scouts and Rangers respectively.

against a wall and throw rocks at them. And he claimed that he had been reincarnated as a goaltender as punishment. He even sometimes went by the nickname "The Count." Gratton was also a believer in astrology, and told Rangers coach John Ferguson one night that he could not play because the stars were not properly aligned. He was the perfect foil for Greg Harrison, who wanted to design something really different.

Gratton lost the game in which he wore three masks, and immediately got on the phone to Harrison about having a new mask made. They talked about doing something with the Rangers colors or logo, but soon settled on a snarling lion because Gratton's astrological sign was Leo.

"I made the mask and I finished it at midnight on a Friday, and from midnight to noon the next day I painted it," Harrison told *Hockey Digest* in 2003. "It took 12 hours just to paint that. It's like an oil painting. I baked it quickly... they flew it to New York, it was there that afternoon, he wore it on a Sunday, and on Monday it was all over the press. It was in *Time* magazine and every newspaper."

Gratton once said that he hoped the mask would frighten opposing shooters—or at least distract them. It didn't work. In 47 NHL games with the Rangers and St. Louis Blues, Gratton had a goals against average of 4.02 and a 13–18–9 record. The lion mask ended up becoming his legacy, and proved a harbinger of things to come in goalie mask art.

With the success and attention given to Gratton's mask, the orders began piling up faster than ever at Greg Harrison's studio. In 1979, he painted an elaborate and ghoulish skull design on a mask he made for Vancouver Canucks goalie Gary "Bones" Bromley. In 1981, in what is still considered one of his masterpieces, Harrison incorporated the Chicago Blackhawks' colorful Indian head logo into a mask design for goalie Murray Bannerman.

While elaborate mask artwork captured the imagination of hockey fans and the sports media, physical design improvements to the fiberglass mask continued to be made by Greg Harrison and mask makers such as Montrealer Michel Lefebvre, who made masks for numerous Quebec-born NHLers, including Michel "Bunny" Larocque, Michel Dion and Richard Sevigny. Like Plante and Homuth before him, Harrison added ridges to the forehead and face of his creations. Both Harrison and Lefebvre extended the chin of their masks downward, sometimes considerably so, to protect the throat area better. The best example can be seen on the Harrison mask worn by St. Louis Blues goalie Mike Liut in the early 1980s. Later, to allow the bottom of the mask to move and give goalies a better view of the pucks at their feet, Harrison added a hinged bib to masks he made for goalies such as Billy Smith of the Islanders and Philadelphia's Wayne Stephenson. The feature was somewhat cumbersome and

Gilles Gratton's snarling lion, another Harrison creation, is among the most popular and compelling masks ever designed.

GREG HARRISON: Mask Maestro

A native of Brampton, Ontario, Greg Harrison combined a love of goaltending and art to become the greatest mask maker and designer of his time, perhaps of all time. As a youngster, he enjoyed wielding a paintbrush every bit as much as a goal stick, and went on to study art and design and play goal at York University in Toronto. Later, even while making masks, Harrison served as a part-time practice goalie for the Toronto Maple Leafs, a vocation that allowed him to extend his list of pro hockey contacts.

In the early 1970s, Harrison met mask maker Roy Weatherbee, who taught him about the properties of fiberglass. In 1973, with a few masks of his own under his belt, Harrison met Pittsburgh Penguins goalie Jim Rutherford at a hockey school run by NHLers Bobby Orr and Mike Walton. For Rutherford, his first NHL customer, he created a mask much like those made by Ernie Higgins. Unlike most mask makers, though, Harrison was not a slave to a particular design. An innovator in every sense of the word, he made masks in many different styles, constantly seeking a better, safer design.

Harrison's first masks were broad and rounded and curved under the chin, while his early 1980s creations, like the mask he made for St. Louis Blues goalie Mike Liut, were narrow with an elongated chin. In the '80s, he made both kinds, creating a rough, weaved finish on his Higgins-like creations (but in a more even and consistent way than Higgins himself did), and a smooth-as-glass finish on the Liut-style ones.

Over the years, Harrison borrowed the strongest elements from masks designed by others, including Jacques Plante's Fibrosport company and Ottawa-based mask maker Jim Homuth, and then improved on them—such as the Fibrosport-esque mask he made for Philadelphia's Pelle Lindbergh. Like Homuth (and unlike Higgins), Harrison used very little padding on the inside of his masks, relying on the sound structure of the mask to absorb and disperse the energy from the impact of the puck.

Harrison had a creative imagination as well. When everyone else was painting logos and team colors, he explored themes tied to players' nicknames and personalities, and painted them with uncanny precision. Even the ventilation holes fit in, never interfering with the design. But even on his most intricate designs, Harrison tried to keep the fan in the arena in mind. He believed that you should be able to make out the detail on the mask from anywhere in the rink. Harrison's masks are among the most recognizable in hockey history, with many of his most famous ones now residing in the hugely popular mask exhibit at the Hockey Hall of Fame, including the notoriously kooky Gilles Gratton's lion mask, Gary Simmons' cobra mask, Gilles Meloche's "heraldry" mask and Murray Bannerman's Blackhawks mask. An artist in every sense of the word, Harrison is the only goalie mask maker ever honored with an art exhibition. In 1981, the McMichael Gallery in Kleinburg, Ontario, featured his work in a juxtaposition of goalie masks and native mask art entitled "Soultenders and Goaltenders."

Harrison was never satisfied in his quest for mask perfection. Still, he may have attained it over 30 years ago when he teamed up with goaltender Dave Dryden to develop the mask and cage combination worn by goaltenders the world over today.

Gilles Gratton wore this Greg Harrison masterpiece in 1976–77, hoping to distract, perhaps even scare, NHL shooters. It didn't work. In fact, the only people he succeeded in frightening were NHL scouts. He played in only one pro game after that season, an AHL loss in which he gave up six goals on 25 shots.

Greg Harrison also designed masks that would help protect the throat, including adding a hinged bib to the mask of Philadelphia's Wayne Stephenson (left). Prior to "going cage," the Islanders' great Billy Smith wore a Harrison design with hinged bib (right).

never really caught on, but led to the development of plastic throat protectors many years later.

THE DOOR TO THE "BIRDCAGE" OPENS

Bill Burchmore's innovative technique of molding a mask to fit a goaltender's face, which allowed facemasks to break through in 1959, also proved to be the fiberglass mask's undoing some two decades later. The fact that the mask fit flush against the face, therefore allowing for better vision, was also its fatal flaw. Goalies' eyes were too close to the eye openings, and were therefore exposed to wayward sticks and the edges of pucks.

Most goalies knew about the molded mask's Achilles heel. In fact, many had played with fire over the years, actually enlarging the eyeholes (usually against the advice of the mask maker) in order to see better. Eye injuries to goaltenders had been occurring at the amateur and minor pro level for years, but NHL netminders had managed to

FOLLOWING PAGES:

Mike Palmateer's Toronto Maple Leafs mask incorporated the team's colors and logo, while Gary Simmons went with Golden Seals green and a striking image that matched his nickname: "Cobra."

Gilles Meloche's Harrison "heraldry" mask was an appropriate coat of arms for the baronesque backstop in Cleveland, while Harrison's Indian head design, created for Chicago's Murray Bannerman, is a classic among mask designs.

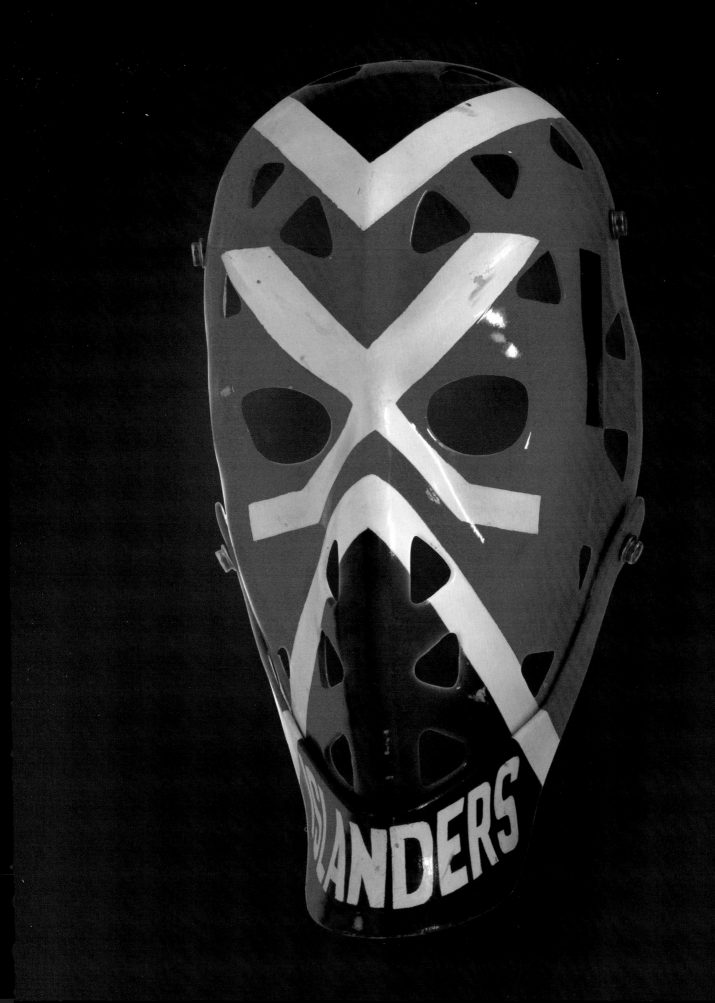

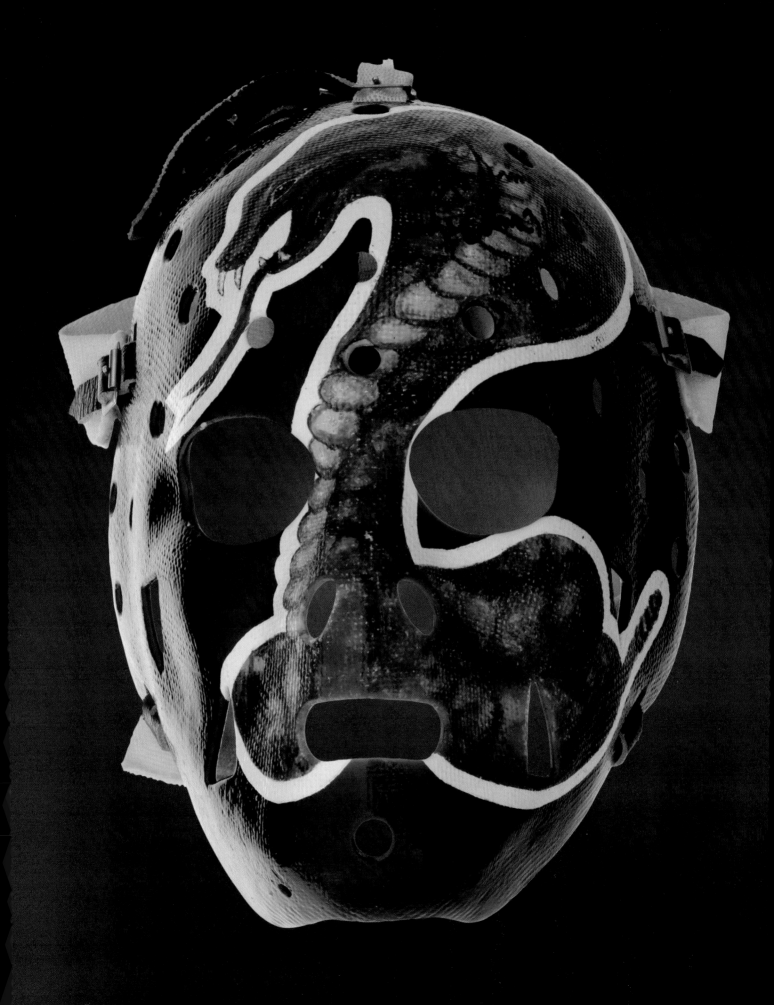

MICHEL LEFEBVRE: Why the Long Face?

Michel Lefebvre didn't only make goalie masks, although that's how he got his start. The Montreal native also designed goalie equipment of all kinds. His pad and glove designs are still used by countless goalies at the amateur and professional level. Lefebvre started making goalie equipment as a hobby when he injured his back and was unable to work. When Montreal-area equipment designer Ted Bourdon had to devote himself to his successful goalie pad business, he contracted out his mask work to Lefebvre.

Lefebvre started out making masks for goalies in the Montreal area and the word about the quality of his work spread quickly. In the 1970s, Lefebvre was the premier mask maker for goalies in Quebec's Junior leagues. Some of his early pro clients included Michel Dion, Sam St. Laurent, Richard Sevigny and Rogie Vachon. Lefebvre's masks had a unique style, with some interesting and innovative design elements. For example, he moved the strap slots and fastening snaps from the edge of the mask toward the temple area, ensuring a snug fit. He also built up the bridge of the nose (as Ernie Higgins did) to protect it from direct impact. Lefebvre's masks were very solid. On his later masks, he increased the size of the circular ventilation holes. And on some masks, such as Michel Dion's, he extended the front ridge down considerably to protect the neck, and moved the chin out so it wouldn't obstruct head movement. The result was an entirely new, immediately recognizable style of mask.

In the 1980s, Lefebvre started to develop his own form of the combination fiberglass mask and cage, or combo, for goaltenders such as Patrick Roy and Mike Liut. Today, along with Greg Harrison, he is considered one of the most influential mask designers of the modern era. Ironically, like Ted Bourdon before him, Lefebvre became so successful making goalie pads and other equipment that he had to leave mask making behind. He eventually passed his mask operations on to a fellow Montrealer, ProtechSport owner Michel Doganieri.

The masks of Montreal mask maker Michel Lefebvre were known both for their extended chins, to protect the throat area, and for the goalies who wore them, often French-Canadians, including Michel Dion, Michel "Bunny" Larocque and Richard Sevigny.

The eye injury suffered by Buffalo's Gerry Desjardins in 1977 helped end the run of the fiberglass molded mask.

Tony Esposito was ahead of his time. He used the Butterfly goaltending technique years before it was popularized in the 1980s and added the cage bars over the eyes of his standard fiberglass mask for better eye protection.

FOLLOWING PAGES:

While Grant Fuhr of the Oilers followed the trend of having masks painted in team colors, Philadelphia's Pelle Lindbergh bucked it, opting for a stark, plain white shield instead.

remain unscathed... for the most part. That changed when a puck clipped the eye of veteran Buffalo goalie Gerry Desjardins in February 1977 and, for all intents and purposes, ended his career. His comeback the following season lasted all of three games.

The Desjardins injury rattled NHL goaltenders. Among those who took note was Chicago Blackhawks Hall of Famer Tony Esposito, who had team trainers add a section of birdcage bars across the eyeholes of his mask. The Canadian Standards Association took note, too. In 1978, the group charged with certifying the safety of sports equipment in Canada banned fiberglass masks from minor hockey. If that decision sounded the death knell for the fiberglass mask, the final nail in its coffin was the career-ending eye injury sustained by Philadelphia Flyers star Bernie Parent in 1979. En masse, NHL goaltenders started turning to the one and only alternative in facial protection, the birdcage mask favored by USSR great Vladislav Tretiak and numerous other amateur netminders the world over. The "cage,"

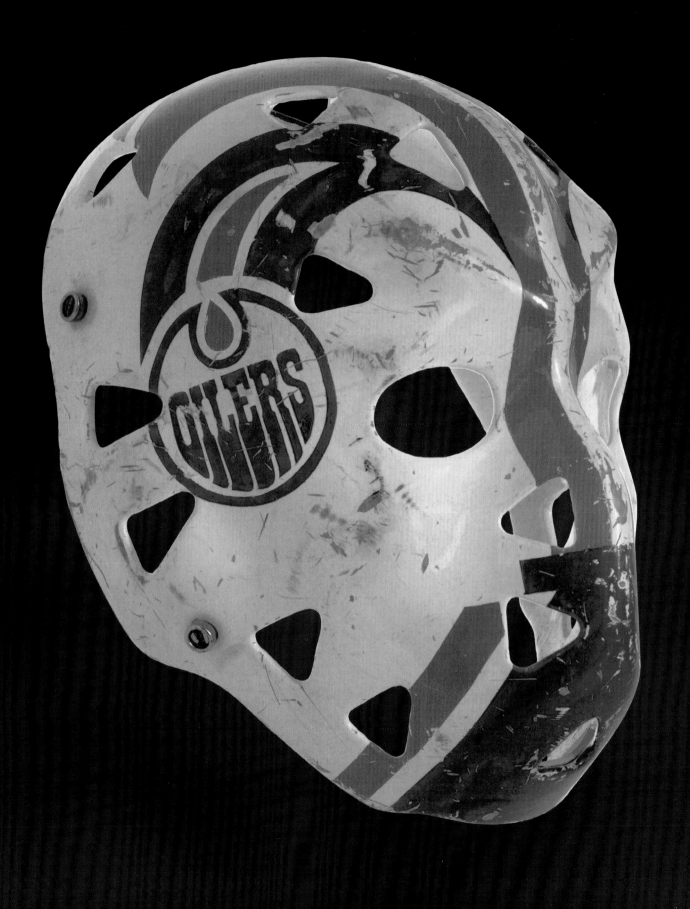

as it came to be known, had actually already been used in an NHL game. Gilles Gratton, the king of the goaltending flakes, wore one for a few games in 1976. After the Desjardins injury, cages appear to have been *de rigueur* in the Buffalo Sabres organization. Desjardins' successor in the Buffalo net was Don Edwards, who wore a Lefty Wilson mask in Junior (his uncle was Detroit goalie Roy Edwards) but switched to a cage shortly after his NHL debut, as did his backup and fellow rookie, Bob Sauve. Longtime mask wearers such as Billy Smith, Chico Resch and Mike Liut switched to the cage, and most of the goalies forced to wear them in Junior kept wearing them once they reached the pros.

By the mid-1980s, only a handful of molded fiberglass mask wearers remained in the NHL. All-Star Pelle Lindbergh of the Flyers wore a plain white Greg Harrison mask until his untimely death in a car accident in 1985, while Sam St. Laurent of Detroit, Chicago's

BIRTH OF THE COMBO MASK

Edmonton Oilers veteran goaltender Dave Dryden knew a thing or two about masks. He made his first one in 1962 while playing senior hockey with the Galt Hornets and later used it in the NHL with the Chicago Blackhawks. Dryden made his second mask in the early '70s when he played for the Buffalo Sabres. He modified this mask several times, sanding it, fixing any cracks or chips and adding a layer or two of fiberglass after each season. He eventually made it bigger so it covered more of his head. Dryden also experimented with other masks, including a Fibrosport model, but he always loved the fit of his home-made design. By 1977, after Gerry Desjardins' eye injury, Dryden was convinced that the cage-style mask was the safest of all. However, Dryden could never get used to the way the helmet fit. He didn't like the way it would move and found it loose and cumbersome. Dryden had the idea to combine the safety of the wire cage with the snug fit of the facemask. He designed a crude version and brought it to mask maker Greg Harrison, whom he had met while having his pads and gloves customized at the Cooper equipment company. Harrison knew exactly what Dryden had in mind and built a fiberglass prototype for Dryden that fit snugly on his face, forehead and chin while the area from the eyes to the mouth protruded and was protected by a cage. The mask was harnessed with a back plate that would move with the goalie's head and neck. The mask and cage combination became known as the "combo." It took several years for NHL goalies to start wearing that design, but once it caught on, it quickly became their mask of choice.

The ongoing quest for greater protection through improved mask design led to the development of the combo mask (above), the choice of almost all goalies today.

The cage became the rage for safety-conscious goalies, including Buffalo's Don Edwards and New York's Gilles Gratton, the first NHLer to wear one.

Murray Bannerman and Warren Skorodenski of the Edmonton Oilers clung to their old-style molded masks as late as 1990.

Many goalies, it turns out, still had a place in their hearts for fiberglass masks. Although cages offered better protection, for the eyes anyhow, they were not much fun to look at. What's more, they could not be colorfully adorned in a team's colors, or personalized in any significant way. What goalies in the 1980s needed was the protection of the cage with the artistic canvas that the fiberglass mask provided. What many didn't know was that one of their own had already teamed up with mask maker Greg Harrison to invent it back in 1977. Once goalies found out about the mask called "the combo," it was the birdcage that was threatened with extinction. The fiberglass mask wasn't dead after all. Like all great and lasting inventions, it was simply changing with the times.

Chapter Four

THE FREEDOM
OF EXPRESSION

THE FREEDOM
OF EXPRESSION

The advent of the helmet and cage interrupted the development of goalie mask art in the late 1970s and early '80s, just when the painting of fiberglass masks was starting to reach its full potential. Once the cage took over, artistic expression on masks was limited to the odd, and rather uninspired, team logo sticker on a helmet.

The combination mask pioneered by Dave Dryden and Greg Harrison in 1977, like the first fiberglass masks, was slow to catch on. But by the mid-1980s more and more professional goalies were wearing it. And thanks to some combo-making pioneers who worked at getting their designs approved by safety regulatory organizations, the combo became available to all goalies, both pro and amateur.

Mask artists were back in business. For if the combo was truly superior in terms of protection, it also provided a blank canvas upon which goalies, through their artist alter egos, could express themselves once again. They didn't disappoint. By the late 1980s, the mask art business was in full swing again, aided this time by advances in paints, tools and techniques. By the 1990s, the transformation was complete, and the results were beyond anyone's wildest dreams. If the goalies that wore the first masks in the early 1960s seemed more like characters in low-budget horror films, modern goalies, with their nearly

Brian Hayward's San Jose Sharks Great White Shark mask has plenty of design bite.

bulletproof high-tech masks and wild airbrush paint jobs, seemed more like masked warriors from a sci-fi blockbuster.

The 1980s were a great time to be a forward… and a hockey fan, too. Pucks filled the net like never before. Scoring records were smashed and 7–5 games were commonplace. But, as goals-against averages from that era show, it was not such a good time to be a goaltender. Goalie equipment had not yet reached the super-sized proportions it would acquire in the 1990s, and goaltending techniques had not kept pace with other changes in the game. The goalie coach was still unheard of, with most netminders of the day having been left to coach themselves from minor hockey on up. The proof can still be seen in the "classic" games from that era replayed on specialty sports TV channels today. In them, players cross the blue line in a flash and let shots rip toward the outside post as the goalie, still a "stand-up" guy for the most part, kicks a skate out in vain. Goalies had a lot of catching up to do.

Now a legendary guru to some of hockey's finest goaltenders, François Allaire was a little-known member of a still-rare species in the mid-1980s—the goalie coach. A former college goaltender himself, Allaire made it his life's mission to learn everything he could about goaltending. By the late 1970s, he was convinced that he had developed the perfect puck-stopping technique—the Butterfly.

Allaire didn't invent the Butterfly. Chicago Blackhawks goalies Glenn Hall and Tony Esposito both employed the knee-knocking technique in the 1960s and '70s. But neither of them did it all the time. And that was the difference: Allaire believed that the Butterfly should be used on every shot on goal: with their hands low and their arms held tightly at their

Patrick Roy's Butterfly positioning helped goaltending emerge from its stand-up style cocoon.

sides, goalies would drop to their knees, using their pads to take away the corners of the net, forcing shooters to try to fit the puck through the small space between the goalie's shoulders and the crossbar above them; the so-called five hole, the space between the goalie's pads when in the Butterfly position, was blocked by his stick.

PUTTING THE COMBO TO THE TEST

Using the Butterfly on every shot called for confidence, not only in the technique, but in the goalie's equipment, too. In the Butterfly position, the goalie's face is directly in the line of fire. Dropping to your knees to face an Al MacInnis slapshot required a really good goalie mask. Fortunately, that mask already existed—although not many goalies were using it yet.

In the summer of 1977, mask maker Greg Harrison built two prototypes of the mask-cage combo he developed with Dave Dryden—one for Dryden himself and the other for Dryden's brother, Ken. Dave tried his with the Edmonton Oilers in a few exhibition games and immediately loved it for its fit. Ken tried his in practices with the Montreal Canadiens, but he was still wearing his standard fiberglass target mask when he retired after the 1979 season.

Like the first fiberglass masks of the early 1960s, the combo mask was slow to catch on. For one, not many people were making them. But for the most part, goalies were simply reluctant to switch from the helmet and cage that many had worn for most of their careers. Like the first masks, it took four or five years from the time Dave Dryden used his in a game for the combo mask to break through. Not surprisingly, the first to adopt the combo were veterans who had used fiberglass masks before. Phil Myre wore his Harrison-made combo with the Philadelphia Flyers as early as 1981, while Chico Resch of the Colorado Rockies and Gilles Meloche of the Minnesota North Stars followed suit shortly thereafter.

The turning point in the popularity of the combo mask came in the spring of 1986, when Patrick Roy, François Allaire's star pupil and the monarch of the Butterfly, led the Montreal Canadiens to a surprise Stanley Cup victory while wearing a plain white combo made by Michel Lefebvre. Edmonton Oilers star Grant Fuhr, wearing a Greg Harrison combo, was the next goalie of note to wear one. The floodgates were now open. By 1987, Greg Harrison had so many customers that he could afford to quit his day job and become a full-time mask maker... and entrepreneur. He called his new business venture simply "The Mask."

By 1988, Harrison's masks were in such high demand that he had to limit his work to professional goalies only. Harrison was a true Renaissance man, combining his talents as a designer, engineer, artist and athlete to create a one-man mask-making enterprise. He took part in every step of the mask-making process, from building the mold to layering up the composite materials. Harrison even welded his own cages. Finally, he cre-

*Colorado Rockies goalie
Chico Resch was an early
adopter of the combo, and
was also quick to add team
colors to his new mask.*

ated the art design, sometimes making preliminary sketches first, and then painting the masks himself. In all, each mask took approximately 40 hours to complete. And each was a veritable work of art, a one-of-a-kind masterpiece that blended function and aesthetics.

THE ARTIST FORMERLY KNOWN AS GILLES... OR EDDIE

It's not necessarily a misconception that a good many goalies were and are "different," solitary figures with a creative, perhaps even artistic, side to them. Gilles Gratton, he of the famous lion mask, for example, was said to be a gifted musician, depending on whom you spoke to, and perhaps who was listening. He was certainly "different," and his mask shows that he had a need to express his individuality. And that was the trouble with the helmet and cage—it couldn't be painted. Standard fiberglass and combo masks, like a blank canvas, provided an artistic outlet for goalies possessing that flair for the creative. For this, goalie masks are unique in all of sport.

Harrison combined a variety of elements in his designs, such as team colors and other, more ethereal symbols that would reveal something about the goalie wearing the mask. The first mask he made for Chicago's Ed Belfour was one of the first cases of true mask personalization. Belfour's teammates called him "Eddie the Eagle," not for his eagle eye in nets, but after bumbling English ski jumper Eddie "The Eagle" Edwards, who soared to fame, if not quite through the air, at the 1988 Calgary Olympics. Harrison transformed the facetious nickname into a persona befitting a masked hockey warrior. He adorned Belfour's brilliant red, black and white mask with a screaming eagle, whose demeanor, he felt, reflected the goalie's own character: proud, courageous, strong, bold... and with keen vision, too.

Other great Harrison masks from the late 1980s and early '90s include the music-themed mask he made for St. Louis Blues goalie Curtis Joseph (before he became Cujo). In blue, white, yellow and red, it featured a clean line graphic of a trumpet on each side and a staff of musical notes on the chin. The full Indian headdress and face paint mask Harrison made for Chicago's Darren Pang was another classic, as were the snarling cat design he came up with for Toronto's Felix "The Cat" Potvin and the mask he made for Winnipeg Jets goalie Bob Essensa, which featured the silhouettes of the famed Avro Arrow fighter jet. Two of Harrison's most striking designs from this time were Don Beaupre's Washington Capitals mask and Jon Casey's North Stars mask, both examples of Harrison's skill at combining color, contrast and clean line graphics recognizable from all vantage points in an arena. Another masterpiece was Tim Cheveldae's Detroit Red Wings mask from 1989, which blended car racing themes and Red Wings graphics.

By 1990, Harrison was overwhelmed by the demand for his masks, and even though he was only making them for professional clients, the

Patrick Roy celebrated the CH
on his Montreal mask.

waiting period for one of his creations was simply too long for many goalies. But Harrison refused to deviate from his time-consuming, hands-on methods and ultimately was unable to keep up with the demand.

THE KING'S MASK MAKER

Fortunately for those who wanted what was now widely considered to be the safest of all goalie masks, others started making "combos." Michel Lefebvre, who first made his mark with more standard fiberglass masks in the late 1970s and early '80s, picked up some of the slack that Harrison couldn't accommodate. In the late 1980s and early '90s he made masks for Mike Liut, Rick Walmsley, Stéphane Beauregard and the great Martin Brodeur. And although he painted simple graphics on some of his earlier masks, by the late 1980s Lefebvre would start sending masks out to be painted.

Most modern goalies change mask makers at some point, and some have had masks made by virtually everyone in the business. But Martin Brodeur and Patrick Roy, two of the game's greatest goalies, remained loyal to Lefebvre-designed masks throughout their entire careers. Roy

FOLLOWING PAGES:

Before adopting the image of his movie mad-dog namesake on his later masks, Curtis "Cujo" Joseph opted for a musical theme on the one he first wore with the St. Louis Blues.

Bob Essensa paid homage to the Avro Arrow fighter plane while with Winnipeg's Jets.

ordered a second mask from Lefebvre for his sophomore season. This new mask extended down to protect more of the neck and jawline and also extended back at the sides so that no part of the head was exposed. This design became Lefebvre's basic custom pro design, although he tweaked it to suit different customers' needs, like Roy's longer-than-most chin.

Roy's mask also featured simple but elegant graphic paintwork—the Canadiens logo on the forehead and three white lines running from the cage to the side of the mask within which the name "Roy" appears. On the chin was Roy's number 33, replacing the "H" in the Canadiens' famous "CH" logo. The mask became Roy's signature during his glory years with the Habs and was one of hockey's most recognizable masks during the early 1990s. When Roy left the Canadiens after his 1995 trade to the Colorado Avalanche, he wore the same Lefebvre-made mask with a new design in Avalanche colors. Martin Brodeur, meanwhile, has kept the same devil design on his Lefebvre mask since 1993. Like Roy's Canadiens mask, it is rather basic and has become Brodeur's on-ice identity. The artwork, in Devils' black and red on white, features part of the team logo on the forehead with subtle flames on the chin and sides.

Roberto Luongo, Jocelyn Thibault and Patrick Lalime have each sported the work of mask maker and fellow Quebecer Michel Lefebvre.

Lefebvre's reputation continued to grow throughout the 1990s with his masks in demand more than ever. But Lefebvre was not only a mask designer; he also became a premier goalie equipment designer. His equipment line became so popular that he was forced to contract out his mask orders to Michel Doganieri, another Montreal-based mask maker who had been making masks since 1988. Today, Doganieri makes all of Lefebvre's pro masks, including those worn by Martin Brodeur, Roberto Luongo, Mathieu Garon, Jocelyn Thibault, Marc Denis, Jean-Sébastien Giguère, Patrick Lalime and Alex Auld. Although he, too, once painted masks, Doganieri's current creations are painted by special mask artists.

NEW FACES

By the end of the 1980s, the combo mask had taken over from the helmet and cage as the leading form of facial protection for pro hockey goalies. One of the first in what would become a new generation of mask makers was New Jersey native Ed Cubberly (see *Look for the "C"*, page 132). Since 1990, he has made masks for NHLers such as Sean Burke, Guy Hebert, Jim Carey, Byron Dafoe, Olaf Kolzig and Tom Barrasso. His most famous mask was created for Mike Richter (page 132).

ED CUBBERLY: Look for the "C"

Ed Cubberly had always been fascinated by the look of goalie masks, especially the contours of the face, and it was this fascination that pulled him into the world of mask design. He got his career started with a late 1970s visit to the Norwood, Massachusetts, shop of mask maker Ernie Higgins to learn the subtleties of the process from the master himself. Cubberly practiced his craft throughout the '80s, researching different composite materials and experimenting with different mask designs until 1988, when he arrived at what he felt was a formula for the ultimate mask. Cubberly's masks are recognizable by the trademark "C" cut in the ear area, helpful for hearing, and for easily identifying their creator. Cubberly's first pro customer was AHL goalie Robb Stauber, in 1989–90. Word of his work spread throughout the minor pro leagues quickly as Ed would hang out in rinks meeting equipment managers and goalies. Soon he had orders from NHL goalies such as Sean Burke, Guy Hebert, Jim Carey, Byron Dafoe, Olaf Kolzig and Tom Barrasso. His most recognizable work is the Lady Liberty mask he made for New York Rangers goalie Mike Richter. Richter was a late convert to the molded mask and when Cubberly delivered his during a Rangers practice, the New York netminder was reluctant to wear it. When practice was over, he had teammate Bernie Nichols line up about 20 pucks and instructed him to shoot them at his head. Richter

Ed Cubberly created the famous Lady Liberty design for one of his most renowned clients, New York's Mike Richter.

removed his gloves, and, with his hands behind his back, made "head butt" type saves with his face. He later told Cubberly that he "just had to know the mask was going to do the job."

Cubberly's proudest moment came in the fall of 1996, when Team USA won the World Cup of Hockey. The team's three goalies, Guy Hebert, Tom Barrasso and Mike Richter, were all wearing masks with a "C" cutout over the ears.

Cubberly's talents were noticed outside of the hockey world, too. In 1991, he made the bite-proof face mask that actor Anthony Hopkins wore to portray the psychotic killer cannibal Hannibal Lecter in the Academy Award®-winning film *The Silence of the Lambs* (see *Masks in the Movies*, opposite page).

Around the same time Ed Cubberly was dreaming of teaming up with the pros, another mask maker had a dream of a different kind—to take the combo mask to the masses. Dundas, Ontario–native Jerry Wright (see *The Wright Mask*, page 135), a self-professed goalie fanatic, made his first mask,

MASKS IN THE MOVIES

What just might be the most famous goalie mask of all was never worn in a hockey game. Horror movie fans know it as the "Jason" mask from the popular *Friday the 13th* movies. The mask was fashioned after an early Fibrosport mask and then, like the murderous Jason character, took on a life of its own.

Jason's first mask was almost certainly store-bought, but other movies have turned to experts for their mask needs. Mask makers Ed Cubberly and Greg Harrison have both contributed their design talents to Hollywood productions. Cubberly designed the mask worn by the evil genius Hannibal Lecter (shown here) in *The Silence of the Lambs*, while Harrison made regular goalie masks for the film *Youngblood* and futuristic-looking masks for the Bob and Doug McKenzie comedy *Strange Brew*. Goalie masks have also been used as disguises by big screen bad guys in action films such as *Heat* and *Exit Wounds*. Gary Smith, the co-author of this book, made replicas of masks worn by Team USA goaltender Jim Craig for the feature film *Miracle*, and by Team Canada goalies Tony Esposito and Ken Dryden for the CBC miniseries *Canada-Russia '72*.

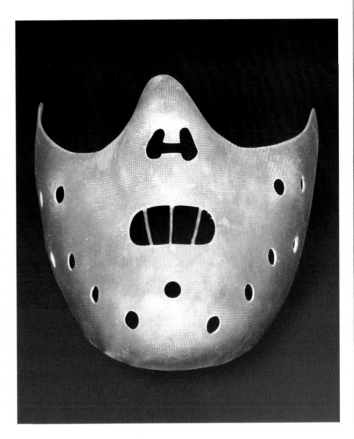

for himself, in 1971. By 1989, he had decided to pursue mask making as a full-time profession. But thinking that the pro market was too difficult to penetrate, he set his sights instead on introducing his combo, the Wright Mask, to the mass market. He cleared his biggest hurdle in 1991, when the Canadian Standards Association approved the Wright Mask for sale in Canada. Soon after, Wright signed on to become the official mask maker for Canadian sporting goods company ITECH with his Wright mask, for all intents and purposes, becoming the ITECH mask.

Six months after being approved by the CSA, the Wright/ITECH mask got its first real breakthrough at the Winter Olympics in Albertville, France, when the spectacular play of American netminder Ray LeBlanc, wearing his Stars and Stripes ITECH mask, turned heads toward his head. In the fall of that year, veteran Ron Hextall, then with the Quebec Nordiques, became the first NHLer to wear an ITECH mask. Before long, Wright was meeting with big-name goalies such as Grant Fuhr and Curtis Joseph, both of whom became clients. Soon, ITECH would become the leading mask manufacturer in the world, and the supplier to hundreds of professional goaltenders.

Other mask makers, such as Don Straus of Armadilla Mask and Eddy Schultz of Eddy Mask—who would go on to make masks for the likes of Mike Vernon, Garth Snow and Manny Legace—were also seeking CSA approval for their mask designs in the early 1990s. Both would make masks for pro goalies and the mass market.

The difference between an approved mask for minor hockey and a pro goalie mask is the cage. Minor hockey goalies have to wear a tight cage with straight bars and smaller openings, while pro goalies can wear a "cat's eye" cage, with curved bars and larger openings in front of the eyes.

Don Straus never played goal, or hockey for that matter. He came to the sport via the world of auto racing. He used his mechanical engineering knowledge to develop a new style of mask, one that was light, cool and impact resistant. Straus' Armadilla masks, bigger and rounder than anything before, marked a real departure from typical combo mask design. And the artwork on them, done by Straus himself, was unique as well. Straus' most famous mask is the one he made for Brian Hayward of the expansion San Jose Sharks in 1991, which is believed to be the first mask painted using the airbrushing technique. Even casual fans remember the gaping jaws of a Great White Shark, which seem to have swallowed Hayward's head whole. Straus also made memorable masks for NHL goalies Kelly Hrudey and John Vanbiesbrouck.

JERRY WRIGHT:
The Wright Mask

Jerry Wright made his first mask for himself in 1971 and continued to perfect his craft throughout the '70s, constantly experimenting with materials and tweaking his design, but never being completely satisfied. By 1981, Wright customers Jim Ralph of the Ottawa 67's and Bruce Dowie of the Toronto Marlboros were the last Major Junior goalies in Ontario wearing the molded fiberglass facemasks. In the late 1980s Wright saw a void in the retail market for combination masks, with which he had started experimenting. In 1989, he decided to leave the security of a government job in order to pursue his passion for mask making. Wright almost lost his nerve. But while waiting to register his business, he saw former NHL goalie Mike Palmateer enter the room he was in. Wright took this as a sign from the hockey gods, and decided to pursue his dream after all.

The Wright Mask, as it was called, differed from other masks in subtle ways. Wright built up the chin area and added a scoop to the bottom, giving the mask a futuristic look. His first mask was marketed as "The Profile I and II." Wright never intended to make masks for pro goalies, but looked to provide masks for minor hockey players instead. Unlike most mask makers, Wright contracted out the manufacturing of the composite shell and assembled the masks himself, churning out up to 10 generic-fitting masks a day. To be able to sell his masks on the mass market, Wright sought approval from the Canadian Standards Association (CSA) and subjected his masks to rigorous testing.

If there was a gold medal for mask design at the 1992 Winter Olympics in Albertville, France, Ray Leblanc's Stars and Stripes mask might have won it.

Wright struggled along at first, selling his product on consignment in a few sporting goods stores in Southern Ontario while advertising in *The Hockey News* with the slogan "Face the Challenge Head On… After all, You've Got an Image to Protect!" Even after teaming up with hockey manufacturer ITECH in 1991, Wright had doubts as to whether he would ever be able to make a living in the retail mask market. In July 1991, Wright received a letter from the CSA informing him that his mask met all safety standards. He knew then that he could step up his production and expand his size range to fit goalies of all ages. The Wright/ITECH mask got its big break in 1992 when Team USA goalie Ray Leblanc wore one in the Winter Olympics in Albertville, France. By 2006, when Wright retired from the mask-making business, no fewer than 35 NHL goalies were wearing his mask.

Another mask maker who emerged in the early 1990s was Dom Malerba, who created the snarling bear mask worn by Boston's Andy Moog. Malerba, who founded his mask company, Pro's Choice, in 1986, has made masks for NHL goalies such as Curtis Joseph, Manny Fernandez and Olaf Kolzig. His current pro masks are marketed under the name Bauer/Nike.

Malerba's association with a large sporting goods manufacturer is not unique. Like Jerry Wright and ITECH, many leading mask makers signed up to work with major equipment makers. Most of these relationships, however, didn't last. Today, it is more common to find mask makers operating their own businesses.

Fit for a King... or a Leaf

Mask maker Matt Garland, whose company, Pro-Masque, makes masks for NHL goalie Dwayne Roloson, had the tradition of mask making handed down to him. His own father made a mask for him back in 1965. Garland, who founded Pro-Masque in the early 1990s, has developed a unique way of fitting goalies for masks. He created what he calls the "Pro Air System," which involves the use of an inflatable air bladder to ensure a perfect fit.

Mask design has certainly come a long way from the days when fitting a mask for a goalie required letting a 20-pound block of plaster harden on

All that glitters...
Kelly Hrudey celebrated Hollywood's glitter on his Kings mask, while John Vanbiesbrouck had his Flyers mask finished with sparkling paint. Both are Armadilla creations (Don Straus).

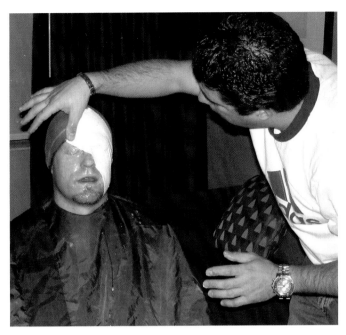

Mask maker Tony Priolo takes a hands-on approach to his craft, here preparing a mold for goalie Tim Thomas. Priolo's mold for netminder Cam Ward is shown at right.

his face. Many modern-day mask makers keep a variety of different sized shells on hand. They choose the one best suited to their customer and then custom fit it. At the retail level, most mask models come in a variety of sizes, and can be fit by customizing the rubber and/or foam padding inside.

Elite goalies, however, generally still sit through a molding session of some kind. Along with the process being less claustrophobic, the materials, too, have changed: Gypsona, a plaster gauze bandage once used by doctors for making casts, has replaced regular plaster, while the use of specialty gels such as alginate (used in dentistry) is common. Once the mold is taken, the mask maker can see the subtleties of the goalie's facial structure and shape the mask shell accordingly.

THE MODERN MASK

The basic design of the combo mask has changed little in 30 years. Even the Harrison-Dryden prototype of 1977 looks a lot like today's masks. The major difference in the modern mask and its precursors is in the materials mask makers now use. Up until the late 1980s, masks were made of fiberglass saturated in either polyester or epoxy resin. Today's masks are both light and extremely resistant to impact because they contain improved composite materials like Kevlar (the same type of material used in

The O'Brien Mask

Before the goalie mask was invented, some amateur goaltenders turned to the catcher's mask for protection. And why not? The catcher's mask, invented by Harvard man Fred Thayer in 1877 (see *Tool of Ingenuity,* page 22), was better than nothing, even if it was meant to protect faces from baseballs and not pucks.

Over 100 years later, the tables were turned, and it is fitting that a change to "America's pastime" was generated from a Canadian city, and by "Canada's game." While watching a hockey game on TV in 1996, Toronto Blue Jays catcher Charlie O'Brien wondered if the cool-looking mask worn by hockey goalies wouldn't offer better protection than the traditional catcher's mask, whose design hadn't changed all that much since Fred Thayer's day. Actually O'Brien did more than wonder—he hooked up with the designers at Van Velden Mask Inc. of Toronto, who took his idea and turned it into the All-Star MVP, a seven-layer-thick shell of fiberglass, Kevlar and other composite materials that looked very much like a typical combo-type goalie mask. Only the cage was different, with a wide horizontal opening for better vision and a chin section that rested atop the shell.

With the approval of Major League Baseball, O'Brien started wearing his mask on May 13, 1997. Scores of big league and Little League catchers soon followed suit.

bulletproof vests) and carbon fiber as well as fiberglass. Sheets of these woven fabrics are saturated with resin, which acts as a glue to bond the different layers together, to form the "shell" of the mask. Although today's mask is nearly indestructible, modern mask makers are continually trying to improve it. In fact, it's not uncommon for mask manufacturers to consult with their design counterparts in the aerospace industry to come up with the formula for stronger, lighter and more impact-resistant masks.

In the combo mask, a steel cage is fastened to the shell. The best cages are stainless steel ones. They have high tensile strength, can be welded easily, and will not rust or corrode. Most mask makers purchase their cages from specialized manufacturers.

Another significant change in mask making has been improvements to the padding inside the mask. Mainly a comfort issue in the old days, foam padding has evolved to play a major safety role, absorbing impact before it can be transferred to the skull.

One designer who has made effective use of the stronger modern materials is Gary Warwick of the Warwick Mask Company, whose masks are renowned for both their strength and lightness. The combo masks Warwick developed in the 1990s, made from carbon fiber and epoxy resin, propelled the company to the top of the list of quality mask makers.

The Port Huron, Michigan–based Warwick began making goalie masks in 1968. In 1979, he was called to Detroit to make a mask for Rogie Vachon of the Red Wings, which marked the beginning of what would be his long association with the team. Today, Warwick masks are worn by an all-star cast of NHL netminders, such as Ryan Miller of the Buffalo Sabres, Marty Turco of the Dallas Stars, Pascal LeClaire of the Columbus Blue Jackets and Evgeni Nabokov of the San Jose Sharks.

One of Warwick's most interesting innovations was the development of a special helmet for Detroit goalie Dominik Hasek. The legendary Dominator, who started his NHL career with a cage fitted to a Cooper SK 2000 helmet back in 1990, remains a dedicated helmet-and-cage man, one of the last of the breed. But after the helmet became hard to find at the end of the '90s, he started experimenting with custom-made, one-piece helmets. In 2001, with the Red Wings, Hasek turned to Warwick, who made him a one-piece helmet out of the same composite materials as his masks. The result was lighter and

more comfortable than anything he had worn before. What's more, it offered a surface that could be painted.

Warwick is part of the long line of mask makers who have taken the mask in new directions over the years, a lineage that now includes Toronto's Tony Priolo. Priolo, who founded his company SportMask in 2002, is known for experimenting with different combinations of composite materials, stainless steel cages, and foam in an effort to make the safest mask ever. He personally tests his masks, donning goalie equipment to stand in front of a puck cannon, which can fire pucks at speeds in excess of 150 kmh (93 mph), aimed at his head. He currently makes standard combo masks for a long list of clients that includes Carolina Hurricanes goalie Cam Ward. But his most famous work is undoubtedly the "Mage" worn by Boston's Tim Thomas. Thomas liked the "old school" helmet-and-cage style of mask, but felt that the helmets lacked durability. Priolo worked at developing this new take on the helmet and cage and called it the Mage, half-mask, half-cage. He recently developed the Mage II, which, unlike its predecessor, features a jaw piece attached to the helmet. The original Mage was basically a molded helmet and cage combination. Dallas Stars prospect Tobias Stephan is another Mage wearer.

HOCKEY'S REMBRANDTS AND PICASSOS

Late in his career, Dominik "the Dominator" Hasek wore a one-of-a-kind helmet and cage design made by the Warwick Mask Company.

While a few mask makers working today still paint their own creations, mask artwork is now mostly the domain of specialists... and they are legion. An Internet search will provide dozens of hits for individuals willing to paint just about anything on masks for goalies of all ages. The most

important mask makers, whether they are large companies or individuals, have artists they can recommend to their customers. Some will go so far as to certify certain artists to paint their products, even voiding the warranties of customers who go elsewhere for a paint job.

A proper paint job can take up to 30 hours to complete, with some more elaborate designs requiring up to 60 hours. Once a concept is sketched out, the prep work begins. This entails sanding the mask down, filling any imperfections and priming the surface. Every painter has his or her own secret formula, the mixing and blending of special paints to produce the brightest colors. The best painters today predominantly use airbrush techniques to create their masterpieces. After the paint is applied, each work is painstakingly clear coated, wet sanded and buffed several times to protect the artwork from chipping and to obtain a high-gloss finish. The cost of a professional paint job ranges from the hundreds to the thousands of dollars.

Most professional goalie masks are painted by a handful of people. One of the premier mask artists working today is Frank Cipra of Prescott, Ontario (see *Hockey Dreams*, page 144), who started out painting masks for local goaltenders in the 1980s. His mask clientele, the first of which included goalies Grant Fuhr and Ron Hextall, reads like a veritable who's who of goaltending. And some of his creations, like the pond hockey mask he painted for Montreal's Jeff Hackett in the mid-1990s, are considered mask art classics. Cipra is currently the official mask painter for ITECH.

Another leading mask artist, Marlene Ross of Brockville, Ontario, was a struggling cartoonist and portrait artist who ventured into the mask art world about 20 years ago. From 1992 to 1995, she worked as a freelance artist in

Part mask, part cage, Tim Thomas' unique Mage was created by Toronto mask maker Tony Priolo.

FRANK CIPRA: Hockey Dreams

Frank Cipra had two passions growing up: hockey and art. And he was pretty good at both. After studying graphic design in college, Cipra was working as a graphic artist in a printing business when he met mask maker Jerry Wright, who would eventually team up with ITECH. Cipra has painted masks for ITECH ever since.

One of Cipra's favorite creations was the mask he painted for Jeff Hackett. When Hackett was traded to the Canadiens, Cipra was having a hard time coming up with a suitable design. So he drew his inspiration from his two sons, who happened to be playing pond hockey in the backyard. The mask, which Cipra called "Hockey Dreams," features two young boys wearing Montreal Canadiens jerseys, toques and scarves playing shinny on a frozen pond.

Cipra is often called upon to paint special masks for goalies who are chosen to represent their countries in international events like the Olympics (if they are wearing ITECH masks). His first international mask was for American Ray Leblanc, who defended the nets of Team USA at the Winter Olympics in 1992. Cipra had only two days to complete the mask, when most of his creations take about 20 to 30 hours to paint depending upon the amount of detail required for the design. It took Cipra two weeks to complete Andrew Raycroft's

Leafs mask, which features Leaf stars of the past as well as Maple Leaf Gardens. Other popular Cipra masks include the unusual "Beer Splash" mask he painted for Ron Tugnutt of the Dallas Stars, a KISS tribute mask for Jamie McLennan, and the current veterans tribute mask worn by Islanders goalie Rick DiPietro.

association with fellow artist Frank Cipra. Ross' first major design job was on the snarling polar bear mask Ron Hextall of the Quebec Nordiques wore in 1992. In 1995, she started Marlene Ross Design, and has since painted masks for leading goalies such as Martin Brodeur, Roberto Luongo, Jean-Sébastien Giguère and José Théodore. Ross has also painted a number of masks used in international competitions, most notably for Team Canada goaltender Martin Brodeur for the 1998, 2002 and 2006 Olympics.

Michigan native Ray Bishop (see *Born to Paint*, page 146) broke into mask painting's big leagues when he approached goalie Jeff Reese of the International Hockey League's Detroit Vipers in 1997. Reese had been

Frank Cipra designed a Leafs' tribute mask for Andrew Raycroft and a maple leaf mask for Team Canada's Kim St-Pierre.

wearing a plain white mask, and Bishop proposed to paint a Medusa design on it. Mask maker Gary Warwick was so impressed with Bishop's work that he started sending him masks to paint. Soon, he was getting calls from the Detroit Red Wings. He has since painted masks for Detroit goalies Manny Legace, Curtis Joseph and Dominik Hasek. In 2001, he painted a mask for St. Louis goalie Fred Brathwaite that featured the character Freddy Krueger from the *Nightmare on Elm Street* horror films. It was the first time that a psychotic serial killer was on a mask, instead of the other way around (see *Masks in the Movies*, page 133).

Another mask artist who can thank Gary Warwick for helping him get his start is Minnesotan Todd Miska (see *Art by Instinct*, page 150). After a recommendation from Warwick, Miska took over the painting of Ed Belfour's eagle designs in 1995. One of his most famous creations is the Gerry Cheevers stitches mask tribute he painted for Boston goalie Steve Shields in 2002. It featured a reproduction of the mask that graces the cover of this book— right down to Gerry's ears and hair sticking out from behind it.

Swedish airbrush artist Dave Gunnarsson got his start painting masks for European league goalies. But his wild and imaginative designs caught on quickly, first with Europeans in the NHL and later with goalies such as Marty Turco, Mike Smith and Tim Thomas.

Gunnarsson is adept at painting everything from gargoyles and mythical beasts to human faces. He has painted tributes to other goalies' masks for Finnish goaltender Hannu Toivonen (Bruins, Blues), including one of

RAY BISHOP: Born to Paint

Unlike Frank Cipra, Ray Bishop never took much interest in hockey while growing up just north of Detroit. But as a child he was always "customizing" his toys, often borrowing his mother's nail polish or white-out to paint his Hot Wheels toy cars. Bishop eventually graduated to model paints, and learned how to prepare surfaces properly so the paint finish would look good. When he was in his early 20s, Bishop purchased his first airbrush and taught himself to use it by painting model cars and T-shirts.

Bishop started to take more notice of hockey around the same time he began working as a painter and auto repair man at a body shop. He eventually struck out on his own, doing graphic design. Word of his talent as an artist started to spread, and not long after he painted his first mask for IHL goalie Jeff Reese in 1997, a number of mask makers started using his services regularly. Detroit Red Wing equipment manager Paul Boyer endorses Bishop as the team's preferred painter, and Bishop has designed mask artwork for several Wings goalies, including Manny Legace, Curtis Joseph and Dominik Hasek.

Bishop has also painted for NHLers such as Roman Turek, and he painted the mask currently worn by Buffalo's Ryan Miller. One of his most popular masks ever was the octopus design he painted for Manny Legace. He also painted Dominik Hasek's current helmet, incorporating a car engine and the winged wheel in the Red Wings logo in a Motor City tribute.

the mask worn by Denis Lemieux, the fictional goalie of the Charlestown Chiefs in the Paul Newman film *Slap Shot*. Gunnarsson has painted masks celebrating Winnipeg-Phoenix franchise greats Dale Hawerchuk, Thomas Steen and Bobby Hull for fellow Swede Mikael Tellqvist of the Coyotes. Earlier, when Tellqvist was a backup in Toronto, he sported a Gunnarsson design bearing the likeness of Leaf great Borje Salming.

THE MEANING OF MASKS

With the advances in airbrushing tools and techniques, today's goalies can have pretty much anything they want painted on a mask... and they do. The NHL gives creative license to the artists and goalies, with a few restrictions. There can be no advertising or statements in poor taste. Although it is not clear that he was forced to discard it, Ottawa Senators goalie Ray Emery (who fancies himself a goalie-pad-wearing pugilist),

Justin Pogge was one in a long line of goalies who wore the maple leaf on their faces in international competition. He wore this mask at the World Junior Championships in 2006, and won gold.

stopped wearing a mask painted by Frank Cipra that depicted controversial boxer Mike Tyson after team and NHL officials sent word that associating a convicted criminal with the game would project the wrong message. Emery has had other boxing-themed masks over the years, including one featuring Canadian boxer George Chuvalo.

The first mask art focused on team colors and logos. Today, personalization, where a goalie's nickname, character or even musical taste is reflected in the artwork, is the most popular mask art theme. Goalies with nicknames like The Eagle, The Cat and Cujo have had ferocious looking beasts painted on their masks. Martin Biron of the Philadelphia Flyers, whose middle name is Gaston, has a goalie stick-wielding lumberjack called The Great Gaston on his current mask. The masks of José Théodore and Marty Turco both fittingly feature gargoyles, the mythical guardians of cities.

There have been masks featuring the rock group KISS, guitarist Jimmy Page, Metallica singer James Hetfield and other rock bands. The smiling face of country singer Garth Brooks is on no less than two masks, including a 2008 Dave Gunnarsson design for country music-loving Montreal Canadiens goalie Carey Price. Goalie Kari Lehtonen of the Atlanta Thrashers has characters from a video game, *Final Fantasy*, on his mask. Enough said.

Other goalies like showing a little civic pride toward the city or region in which they play. Many have landmarks and even landscapes on their masks. John Grahame of the Carolina Hurricanes has a NASCAR racing theme on his, complete with a busty, bikini-wearing NASCAR fan.

Yes, like conventional art, mask art is definitely a matter of taste.

"Holy hockey puck, Batman...," Pittsburgh goalie Ken Wregget's mask featured a penguin of another kind.

TODD MISKA: Art by Instinct

As a child growing up in Minnesota, Todd Miska always loved to draw, but had little formal training. Miska started working in a sign shop after graduating from high school, and it was there that he learned to airbrush. Relying on his instinct for color, contrast and composition, he developed his own unique style of mask art. Miska painted his first mask for a local goalie when he was only 14 years old while working at a sporting goods store. After his first customer attended a goalie school in the summer, Miska's name spread via word of mouth.

Miska now paints goalie masks full time, with an assistant helping him in his shop. Among the more popular masks he has created in recent years are the Gerry Cheevers tribute mask worn by Steve Shields, the skull mask worn by Calgary's Miikka Kiprusoff and the gruesome sea creature mask of San Jose Sharks goalie Evgeni Nabokov. He has also painted masks for Ed Belfour, Josh Harding, Nicklas Backstrom and Manny Fernandez.

MASKS WITH A MESSAGE

The small area on the chin of the mask is a great place for a jersey number or team or player nickname—such as "Habs," "Bulin Wall," or "Kipper." When he was with the Montreal Canadiens, Swiss goalie David Abeischer had a Quebec provincial license plate with his nickname, "Abby," on the chin of his mask. The same goes for the mask's back plate, which is often used for nicknames and special messages. Many players have their children's names or initials back there for good luck. Ryan Miller of the Buffalo Sabres has "Matt Man" on the back of his in remembrance of a young cousin who lost a battle with leukemia. Sometimes the entire design contains a message. New York Islanders goalie Rick DiPietro, whose father was a Vietnam War veteran, had Frank Cipra paint him a highly patriotic mask honoring American veterans. In 2007, Josh Harding of the Minnesota Wild had a mask painted with a large pink ribbon and the

Olaf Kolzig of the Washington Capitals, whose son Carson is autistic, has the Athletes Against Autism logo painted on his back plate.

messages "Fund the Fight" and "Find a Cure" after his sister Stephanie was diagnosed with breast cancer.

Another mask design phenomenon is the painting of tribute masks and masks to mark special occasions. Toronto goalie Curtis Joseph put aside his snarling Cujo mask for the closing of Maple Leaf Gardens in 1999. For that one game only, he wore a mask featuring an artist's rendering of the Gardens, various Leafs logos, and the message "Memories and Dreams 1931–1999." Jocelyn Thibault's mask with Montreal recreated Jacques Plante's famous pretzel mask… or tried to, anyway. And Todd Miska's Gerry Cheevers mask for Steve Shields took that idea one step further, even adding ears and hair. Dave Gunnarsson has made at least two similar tribute masks for goaltender Hannu Toivonen, including one reproducing a mask worn by St. Louis Blues goalie Ed Staniowski in the late 1970s.

The ultimate goalie tribute mask, however, has to be the one Worcester, Massachusetts–based mask artist Mike Myers painted for Josh Harding. It depicts classic goalie masks worn by Jacques Plante, Ken Dryden, Mike Liut, Gerry Cheevers, Tony Esposito, Terry Sawchuk, Pelle Lindbergh, Cesare Maniago, Ed Giacomin and Bunny Larocque.

A mask about masks? Masks with ears and hair? Where does mask art go from here? Anything, it seems, can now be reproduced on a mask. Maybe a hint as to a future direction of mask art was delivered by goalies Martin Biron and Martin Gerber, who in recent seasons have worn a plain white and plain black mask respectively. But it isn't likely. These were surely subtle "trade me, please" messages rather than art criticism. Perhaps it is best that today's mask artists continue to find their inspiration in the often quirky nature of their clients, a source, it would seem, of endless surprises.

As for the mask itself, just like the first masks of nearly half a century ago, developments in hockey will dictate the level of protection goalies will need. One thing is certain, the masks worn by modern goalies must be, first and foremost, strong. Sticks have been designed to shoot pucks at speeds once thought unreachable, by players stronger and faster than their 1960s predecessors.

Improvements to equipment, training and overall athletic fitness will continue. For that is the nature of competition, to win… and keep winning. And the modern hockey player is a warrior bred to compete… hard. But there are many reasons for goalies to be hopeful in regard to their future safety, especially with the vigilant crop of current mask makers on the job, and more on their way. The mask used by professional goalies today is the result of nearly 50 years of technological advances in the materials used to create them. Further improvements, including better materials and testing tools, are being made every day in the name of safety. The game of hockey is now played with nearly unthinkable power and speed, yet facial injuries to goaltenders are quite rare. The goalie's mask, his "saving face", is doing its job more effectively than ever before. And there is every reason to believe that it will only get better.

Josh Harding's mask of masks is the ultimate tribute to hockey's greatest goalies... and greatest masks.

Index

Picture Credits

6   Mecca/Hockey Hall of Fame

8   Erich Lessing/Art Resource, NY

10–11 *(From left to right)* Bildarchiv Preussischer Kulturbesitz/Art
     Resource, NY; Erich Lessing/Art Resource, NY; Digital Image
     © The Museum of Modern Art/Licensed by SCALA/
     Art Resource, NY; iStockphoto; [Value Stock Images]/
     Unlisted Images, Inc.

12   James Rice/Hockey Hall of Fame

14   Musée McCord, VIEW-3485.0

16   James Rice/Hockey Hall of Fame

17   Hockey Hall of Fame

19   James Rice/Hockey Hall of Fame

20   *(Top left)* Hockey Hall of Fame

20   *(Top right)* Hockey Hall of Fame

20   *(Bottom)* Matthew Manor/Hockey Hall of Fame

21   Hockey Hall of Fame

22   National Baseball Hall of Fame Library, Cooperstown, NY

24   Imperial Oil-Turofsky/Hockey Hall of Fame

25   *(Left)* Imperial Oil-Turofsky/Hockey Hall of Fame

25   *(Top right)* Imperial Oil-Turofsky/Hockey Hall of Fame

25   *(Bottom right)* Imperial Oil-Turofsky/Hockey Hall of Fame

26   Imperial Oil-Turofsky/Hockey Hall of Fame

27   Imperial Oil-Turofsky/Hockey Hall of Fame

28   *(Left)* The Gazette (Montreal)

28   *(Right)* Imperial Oil-Turofsky/Hockey Hall of Fame

29   Imperial Oil-Turofsky/Hockey Hall of Fame

30   Time & Life Pictures/Getty Images
     (photographer: Ralph Morse/Stringer)

31   Imperial Oil-Turofsky/Hockey Hall of Fame

32   Michael Burns Sr./Hockey Hall of Fame

33   Imperial Oil-Turofsky/Hockey Hall of Fame

36   The Gazette (Montreal)

38   *(Top)* Frank Prazak/Hockey Hall of Fame

38   *(Bottom)* ©Bettman/CORBIS

39   Imperial Oil-Turofsky/Hockey Hall of Fame

40   Matthew Manor/Hockey Hall of Fame

42   Matthew Manor/Hockey Hall of Fame

44   The Gazette (Montreal)

45   Imperial Oil-Turofsky/Hockey Hall of Fame

46   *(Left)* Imperial Oil-Turofsky/Hockey Hall of Fame

46   *(Right)* Imperial Oil-Turofsky/Hockey Hall of Fame

47   Imperial Oil-Turofsky/Hockey Hall of Fame

48   Imperial Oil-Turofsky/Hockey Hall of Fame

49   Imperial Oil-Turofsky/Hockey Hall of Fame

50   Frank Prazak/Hockey Hall of Fame

51   Imperial Oil-Turofsky/Hockey Hall of Fame

52   Imperial Oil-Turofsky/Hockey Hall of Fame

53   Imperial Oil-Turofsky/Hockey Hall of Fame

54   Imperial Oil-Turofsky/Hockey Hall of Fame

55   Frank Prazak/Hockey Hall of Fame

56   *(Left)* Imperial Oil-Turofsky/Hockey Hall of Fame

56   *(Right)* Imperial Oil-Turofsky/Hockey Hall of Fame

57   Matthew Manor/Hockey Hall of Fame

59   *(Left)* Imperial Oil-Turofsky/Hockey Hall of Fame

59   *(Right)* Graphic Artists/Hockey Hall of Fame

60   *(Top left)* Graphic Artists/Hockey Hall of Fame

60   *(Top right)* Portnoy/Hockey Hall of Fame

60   *(Bottom left)* Robert Shaver/Hockey Hall of Fame

60   *(Bottom right)* Graphic Artists/Hockey Hall of Fame

62   Portnoy/Hockey Hall of Fame

63   Portnoy/Hockey Hall of Fame

64   Bill Ryerson/Boston Globe/Landov

65   Dan Goshtigian/Boston Globe/Landov

66   Matthew Manor/Hockey Hall of Fame

67   Graphic Artists/Hockey Hall of Fame

68   Graphic Artists/Hockey Hall of Fame

69   Portnoy/Hockey Hall of Fame

70   Frank Prazak/Hockey Hall of Fame

71   Matthew Manor/Hockey Hall of Fame

72   Portnoy/Hockey Hall of Fame

73   Frank Prazak/Hockey Hall of Fame

75   Jim Sanderson

76   Portnoy/Hockey Hall of Fame

77   O-Pee-Chee/Hockey Hall of Fame

79   Frank Prazak/Hockey Hall of Fame

80   Matthew Manor/Hockey Hall of Fame

81   Portnoy/Hockey Hall of Fame

Acknowledgments:

The authors, editors and designers wish to thank the
following individuals for their help on the book:

Tony Accordino, Salma Belhaffaf, Ray Bishop, Dave Britt, Robb Bromley,
John Brown, Steve Cardillo, Gerry Cheevers (www.gerrycheevers.com),
Ed Cubberly, Frank Cipra, Michel Doganieri, Pierre Home-Douglas,
Dave Dryden, Red Fisher, Matt Garland, Ed Giacomin, Rob Harris, Brian
Hedberg, Jim Homuth, Dick Irvin Jr., Christopher Jackson, Steve Jaspens,
Kirk Jennison, Mary-Margaret Klempa, Jeff Kroze, Nicole Langlois,
Irene Lavertu, Tom Lawson, Michel Lefebvre, Maria MacDonald,
Cesare Maniago, Seth Martin, Todd Miska, Michael Myers,
Dave Neuman, John Pothitos, Tony Priolo, Domenic Scalia, Remo Scappaticci,
Gerry Schultz, Dennis Simone, Lissa Smith, C.A. Stacey, Doug Sweet,
Nelson White, Ross "Lefty" Wilson, Jerry Wright, Judy Yelon.

A special thank you goes to Craig Campbell, Manager, Resource Centre and
Archives, Hockey Hall of Fame, and to the team at the Hall, for their invaluable
support and for providing access to a treasure trove of hockey images.